Woodworking Projects with Power Tools

Woodworking Projects with Power Tools

John Sainsbury

Sterling Publishing Co., Inc. New York

Distributed in the U.K. bv Blandford Press

Edited and designed by Hannah Reich

Library of Congress Cataloging in Publication Data

Sainsbury, John A.
    Woodworking projects with power tools.

    Bibliography: p.
    Includes index.
    1. Woodwork.   2. Power tools.   I. Title.
TT180.S328   1983   684'.083   83-12349
ISBN 0-8069-7780-9 (pbk.)

Second Printing, 1984

Copyright © 1983 by John Sainsbury
Published by Sterling Publishing Co., Inc.
Two Park Avenue, New York, N.Y. 10016
Distributed in Australia by Oak Tree Press Co., Ltd.
P.O. Box K514 Haymarket, Sydney 2000, N.S.W.
Distributed in the United Kingdom by Blandford Press
Link House, West Street, Poole, Dorset BH15 1LL, England
Distributed in Canada by Oak Tree Press Ltd.
% Canadian Manda Group, P.O. Box 920, Station U
Toronto, Ontario, Canada M8Z 5P9
Manufactured in the United States of America

CONTENTS

ACKNOWLEDGMENTS

My grateful thanks to Tony Walker, of Bahco Record, Sheffield, England, for his drawings on page 16, his enthusiasm, and his company's permission to use some of the photographs in this book; to the craftsmen whose work is shown on pages 159–187; to the Coronet Tool Company, Craft Supplies of Millers Dale, Rhodes Flamefast, Ltd., W. G. Ball, Enamel Manufacturers, and W. L. Fuller, Inc.

Thanks also to Beth Flowerday, for her endless patience and her care in typing my manuscript, and to my wife, for ignoring the many household jobs I never found time to do.

Illustrations 11, 270, and 271 photographed by Geoffrey B. Platts; illustrations 296 and 298 by A. Seaman & Sons.

INTRODUCTION

This book will be an adventure in wood. Wood, one of the most beautiful raw materials, is found in many different forms—some natural, some man-made. It will dominate our creative activity.

Wood in all its forms can be used: Shavings, sawdust, veneers, tree limbs, stumps from the fire, roots, wood washed up on the shore, offcuts, scrap furniture are all possibilities.

Many of the projects will offer creative use of small pieces of sawn timber. As a result, domestic timbers—timbers of the garden and hedgerow—can be seasoned and used. Many beautiful woods only available in small sizes and often discarded because of this can be used with less attractive ones.

Making up wood from scrap veneers and veneer-and-wood layers will provide opportunity for adventure in form and design.

A wide range of machine tools is now readily available. They are priced within the reach of the hobbyist. School workshops are also equipped with an ever-widening range of machine tools. Creativity with wood, therefore, can be experienced using this variety of machine equipment.

I hope that this book will appeal to woodworkers of all ages and all levels of expertise.

METRIC EQUIVALENCY CHART

MM—MILLIMETRES   CM—CENTIMETRES

INCHES TO MILLIMETRES AND CENTIMETRES

INCHES	MM	CM	INCHES	CM	INCHES	CM
⅛	3	0.3	9	22.9	30	76.2
¼	6	0.6	10	25.4	31	78.7
⅜	10	1.0	11	27.9	32	81.3
½	13	1.3	12	30.5	33	83.8
⅝	16	1.6	13	33.0	34	86.4
¾	19	1.9	14	35.6	35	88.9
⅞	22	2.2	15	38.1	36	91.4
1	25	2.5	16	40.6	37	94.0
1¼	32	3.2	17	43.2	38	96.5
1½	38	3.8	18	45.7	39	99.1
1¾	44	4.4	19	48.3	40	101.6
2	51	5.1	20	50.8	41	104.1
2½	64	6.4	21	53.3	42	106.7
3	76	7.6	22	55.9	43	109.2
3½	89	8.9	23	58.4	44	111.8
4	102	10.2	24	61.0	45	114.3
4½	114	11.4	25	63.5	46	116.8
5	127	12.7	26	66.0	47	119.4
6	152	15.2	27	68.6	48	121.9
7	178	17.8	28	71.1	49	124.5
8	203	20.3	29	73.7	50	127.0

Illus. 1. Costume jewelry with veneer laminates and veneers laid on end as line stringing.

COSTUME JEWELRY

Many attractive items of costume jewelry, such as cuff links, brooches, rings, pendants, earrings, buttons, and tie clips can be made from small, pleasing pieces of wood (Illus. 2). By using machine-boring tools in the standard pedestal drill (or the electric drill in a drill stand), wood can be fashioned with forms based largely on the circle and the straight line (Illus. 3–9). Woods can be chosen in colors that match the article of clothing that the jewelry will accompany.

Illus. 2. Many different-colored woods with a variety of inlaid plugs.

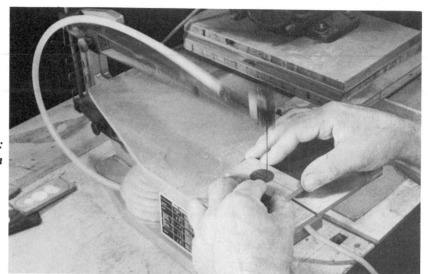

Illus. 3. Making a brooch: Using a Hegner saw to cut an inlaid piece in half.

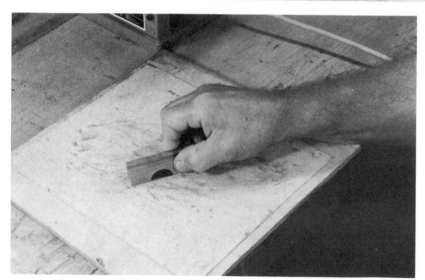

Illus. 4. Truing up the faces on an abrasive board fitted with very fine sandpaper (glass paper).

Illus. 5. Gluing pieces together to form a new design.

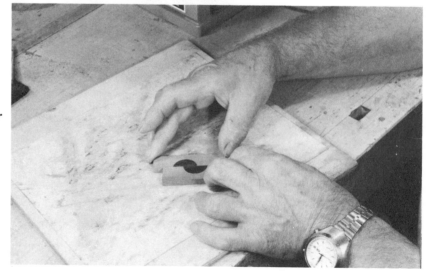

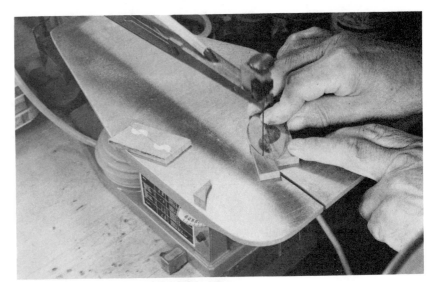

Illus. 6. Shaping the piece with the jigsaw.

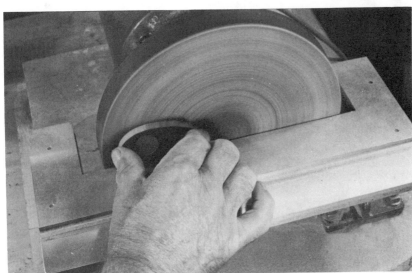

Illus. 7. Another piece in progress: Sanding to shape with a disc sander.

Illus. 8. Further shaping.

Illus. 9. Final finishing on an abrasive board.

Many attractive materials can be used as fillings and inlays (Illus. 10). Jeweler's findings are available in brass, nickel, silver, and gold (Illus. 11).

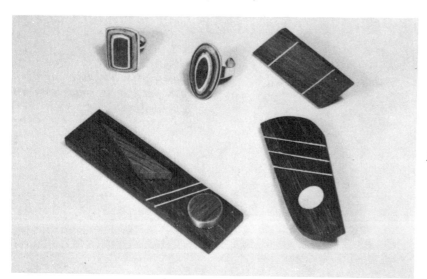

Illus. 10. Finished jewelry.

Illus. 11. Jewelry findings.

Illus. 12. Costume jewelry.

Tools and Materials

Plugs up to 1½-inch (38.1-mm) wide can be cut from suitable wood using tube-type plug cutters. Shallow holes cut with Forstner or sawtooth cutters will be the perfect size. The lines that show on the finished work will be very high quality, because of the excellence of the cut (Illus. 12). Tiny holes are best cut with lip and spur bits or woodworker's drills. Grooves to receive veneers laid edge-on are cut using a dovetail saw, or any saw with very fine teeth. Stringings and bandings are also cut in this fashion. Use a hollow mortise chisel to cut square holes.

Plugs and veneers can be glued using P.V.A. glue or other woodworking adhesive. Sawdust and metal chips and fillings mixed with an epoxy resin glue may be used as a filler (Illus. 13–17). This filler is filed or rubbed down on an abrasive board when dry. Metal wire, strip solder, knots, and plastics can be similarly affixed. Enamelled discs, tumbled stones, thinly cut stone, and cabochons are secured with an epoxy resin glue.

Illus. 13. Inlaying with sawdust: wood dust will be mixed with two-part epoxy-resin glue.

Illus. 14. Mixing the two-part glue.

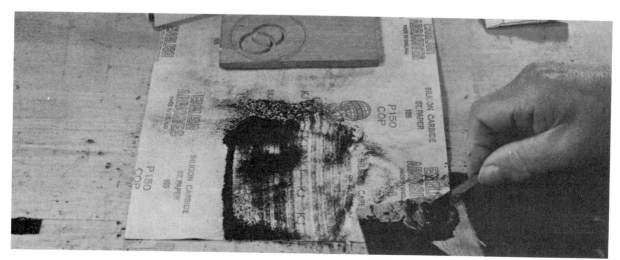

Illus. 15. Mixing the sawdust with the glue.

Illus. 16. Filling recesses cut with a plug cutter.

Plug Cutters

It is essential when working with tools to be sure that the work is held securely at all times. This is especially true when using the plug cutter. This tool can only be used in the machine drill, and the work being cut must be held securely in a vise. See Appendix E for two possible ways to hold work, and for possible additions to the woodworker's vise that will make it easier to hold round or awkwardly shaped pieces. One involves recesses cut in the cheeks of the vise, which thereby hold oddly shaped pieces of wood safely and securely.

Illus. 17. With the filling dry and the surplus removed, the piece is ready for shaping.

Design Suggestions

Examples of the following design possibilities are illustrated in Illus. 18.

> Simple plug inlays
> Plugs inlaid with other plugs
> Plugs inlaid with veneer or stringing
> Plugs inlaid with plugs inlaid with veneers
> Plugs inlaid with plugs inlaid with sheet metal or wire
> Off-center inlays in plugs
> Plugs inlaid with fillings in grooves, or in round or square holes
> Plugs decorated with plug grooves
> Plugs inlaid with tube and filled
> Plugs inlaid, split, and reassembled off-center
> Plugs inlaid, split, and laid
> Plugs laid on each other
> Plugs joined to each other edge to edge
> Plug pairs of contrasting woods split and reglued edge to edge
> Plugs inlaid with veneer laminates

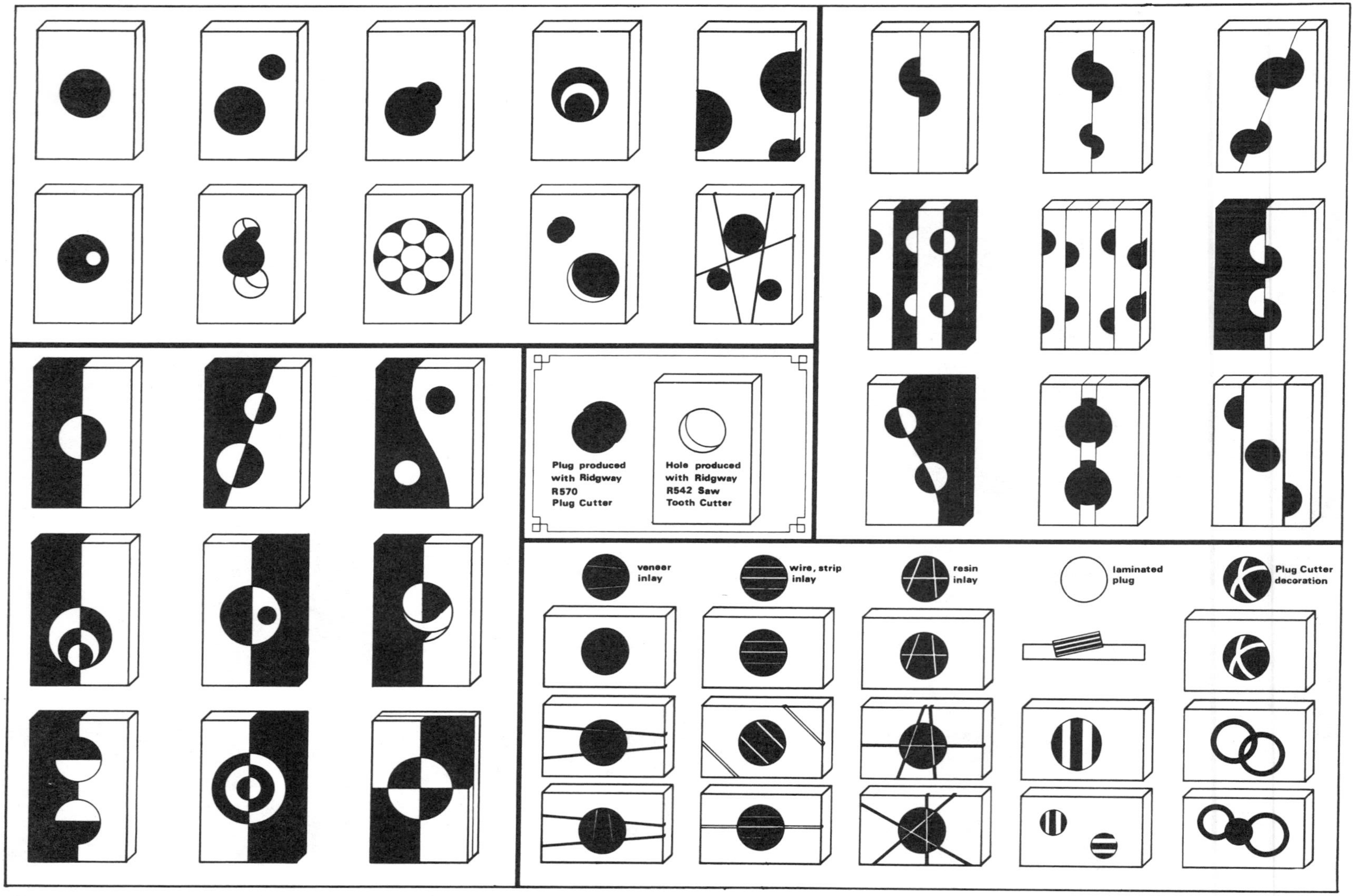
Plug produced
with Ridgway
R570
Plug Cutter
Hole produced
with Ridgway
R542 Saw
Tooth Cutter
veneer
inlay
wire, strip
inlay
resin
inlay
laminated
plug
Plug Cutter
decoration

Illus. 18. Sample designs. Use exotic woods for heightened effect.

Illus. 19. Bangle in rosewood and sycamore.

TURNED BRACELETS AND BANGLES

Many beautiful bracelets can be fashioned using small pieces of exotic wood and other materials. Where veneers are used, they need to be thick. I usually saw these up to suit the particular project. Laminations give great strength and stability to this type of work, as well as offering an almost limitless variety of design options. Inserts of ivory, silver wire, bone, horn, and other material can be applied with considerable success.

First, prepare veneers or thinly cut woods of contrasting colors. For successful finishing, take care to match them for hardness. Glue up, moving each laminate through 90° to add to the stability of the completed lamination. Allow a considerable length of time for drying. When dry, mark up and cut on the band saw or jig saw.

Several methods can be used to mount the work on the lathe (Illus. 20–22). Alternatively, the complete job can be worked by hand. Boring of the side, edge, or inset holes can be done *in situ* on the lathe or on the drill press. In the latter case, careful marking out and safe holding are crucial. Once again, the wooden vice should be pressed into use.

Attaching the Work to the Lathe

Perhaps the easiest way is to mount the laminate to a glue chuck attached to a screw chuck. The glue chuck woodblock should be slightly

Illus. 20. Making a maple and Indian rosewood bangle: Woods are glued and then bored with a plug cutter. They are then ready to be mounted to a collet chuck.

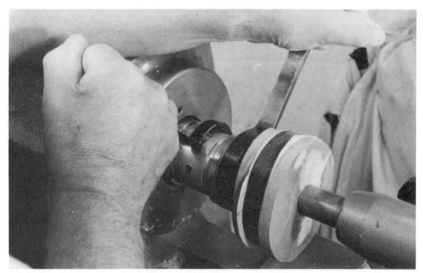

Illus. 21. Tightening the chuck with a C-spanner. The block is held in place by the tailstock quill.

Illus. 22. Turning a bangle to shape.

less wide than the inside diameter of the finished bracelet or bangle. Ideally, it should be a fairly thick wood, to provide space for easy tooling between the headstock of the lathe and the work.

Making the Bracelet

With the work attached in this way, turn down to round (Illus. 24–25). If the edge, face inserts, or plugs are to be made of other materials, set up the dividing head and boring attachment (pages 82–83). Bore holes as necessary, glue plugs, and insert. Turn down carefully from both faces, and cut the inside edge as far as possible. Completely finish the outside, polishing it to a hard, matte finish. Carefully part off through to the glue chuck and complete the inside (Illus. 26–27).

Place another block that is larger than the outside diameter of the bangle on the screw chuck. Cut a sufficiently large recess in this block to provide a push-fit for the bangle.

Trim and polish the inside. To complete, remove and reverse the bangle. Alternatively, if a sawtooth cutter of the correct size is available, the bangle could be parted off with it.

Illus. 23. Finished bangle.

Illus. 24. Removing the waste and squaring the inside.

Illus. 25. Finishing the inside.

19

Illus. 26. Shaping.

Illus. 27. Cutting to the desired internal diameter with a parting tool.

Another Method

The basic block can be bored first, and then mounted onto a tapered wooden mandrel. This can be a block held on either a faceplate or a screw chuck. It can also be a tapered mandrel driven between centers. Take care to keep the work square on the mandrel if this latter method is used. If inserts will be made, bore them first.

Illus. 28. Completed bangle in palisander.

Illus. 29. Mandrel with arbor being inserted in the lathe. The block has been bored and is ready to slide on.

Illus. 30. Block in position on the mandrel.

Illus. 31. Block fixed to a threaded steel mandrel that has a Morse taper, for inserting into the headstock.

Illus. 32. Bringing up the running center to accommodate the right-hand countersunk end of the mandrel.

Illus. 33. Marking out with a parting tool.

Illus. 34. Shaping with the ¼-inch (6-mm) roundnose gouge from the right.

Illus. 35. Shaping from the left.

Illus. 36. Parting off.

Illus. 37. Palisander ring with plug insert.

Illus. 38. Plug insert being held in place by wedge while wood block is bored.

Illus. 39. Prepared block being mounted on the pin mandrel.

Illus. 40. Block assembled and ready for turning.

Illus. 41. Shaping the ring.

Illus. 42. Squaring the ends with the skew chisel.

Illus. 43. Burnishing with a wooden stick.

Illus. 44. Box in olive ash. Turned lid of bog oak with inlaid holly plug.

Illus. 45. Box in bird's eye box inlaid with tulipwood. Turned lid of palisander.

JEWELRY BOXES

Numerous variations can be worked out, but basically, a jewelry box consists of a box that has been bored out using a sawtooth machine cutter, or a machine Forstner bit if the boring is not too deep. (See pages 146–147 for information on sawtooth and Forstner machine bits.)

Lids can be constructed of plugs cut with the plug cutter, or they can be turned on the lathe. Both lid and body can be designed with plugs and veneers used as lines (Illus. 44–45). In fact, stringings and bandings can be purchased and used variously. The shape of the box can be any geometrical figure—square, round, or anything in between (Illus. 46).

Illus. 46. Jewelry boxes in the making.

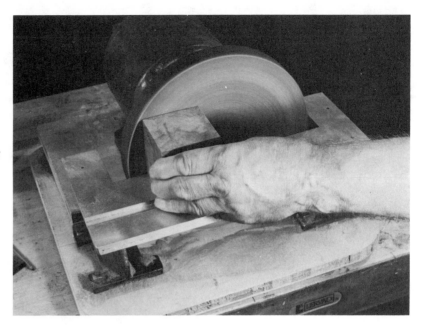

Illus. 47. Cleaning a cube using the disc sander.

Box bodies are prepared on the bench. Perfect finish is obtained with an abrasive board or with an abrasive disc on the sanding machine (Illus. 47). Boring is best done on the drill press. A means of holding the block safely and without damage is necessary (Illus. 48). (Refer to pages 136–140 for information about work-holding aids and the devices used for hand- and vise-holding of parts to be bored.)

When boring, always consult a speed table. Before beginning, adjust the speed of the drill press to suit the size of the hole to be made. It is possible also to bore a block of wood first and then attach it to the lathe with a pin mandrel. This technique permits boxes to be partially turned, completely turned, or offset.

Illus. 48 (below left). Boring a box block with a wood vise. Block is held in place with folding wedges.

Illus. 49 (below right). Completely bored block. Shavings cleared away to show method of holding.

Illus. 50. Holding a block in the machine vise for boring. Sliding jaw has been removed and wood block substituted, to give added space.

Illus. 51. Machine vise with wood jaws added to protect work. Small block is held in v-shaped indentations for boring.

Illus. 52. Hand vise holding small block between folding wedges.

Using Exotic Woods and Inlays

Inserts of exotic woods, plain metal, coins, or enamelled metal provide jewelry boxes with great variation (Illus. 53–54). Measure enamelied discs exactly before boring, otherwise hard glaze will have to be removed from the enamel discs to make them fit. Inserts can be fixed in place with epoxy glue. For information on using sheet silver or silver wire, and on making enamelled discs and other inserts, see pages 113–119.

Illus. 53 (right). Tiny ring box in cocobolo with coin inlaid in lid.

Illus. 54 (below). Possible uses of plug and veneer inlays.

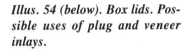

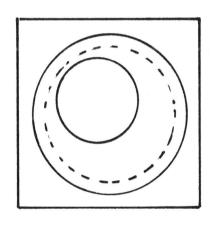

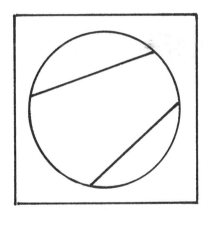

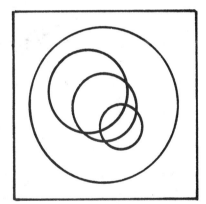

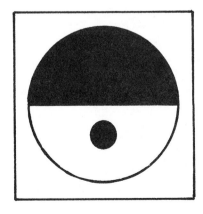

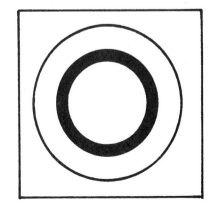

Illus. 55. Holly box with inlaid cabochon.

Using Tumbled Stones and Cabochons

Cabochons make extremely attractive additions to boxes when they are chosen carefully to contrast dramatically with the woods used for the box bodies. Slab work offers many color variations, and slabs can be cut easily and ground to fit into both round and square recesses.

Illus. 56. Suggestions for inlaid plug decorations for sides of boxes.

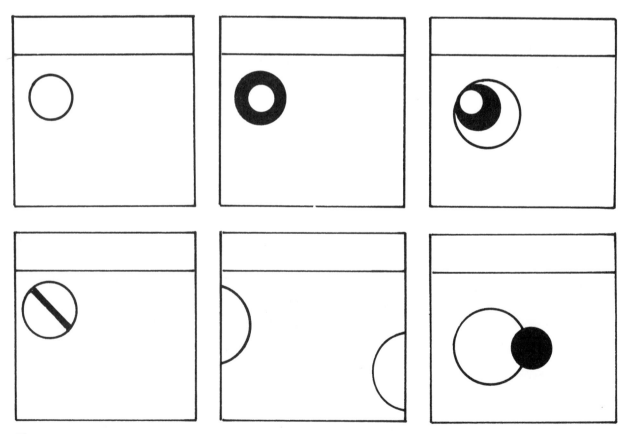

Illus. 57. Sycamore box with etched slate insert in the lid.

TURNED MINIATURE BOXES

Miniature boxes are a great use for odd pieces of fruit woods and unusual scraps of wood that are more often than not discarded. Many beautiful designs can be conceived by mixing woods, using their flaws, and just having fun.

The wood is first mounted on a screw chuck, pre-bored, and then mounted on a pin mandrel or a prepared wood mandrel (Illus. 58–63).

Illus. 58. Making a box in pitch pine: The pre-bored block is ready for assembling to the pin mandrel.

Illus. 59. Turning the block to round, and squaring the base with a skew chisel.

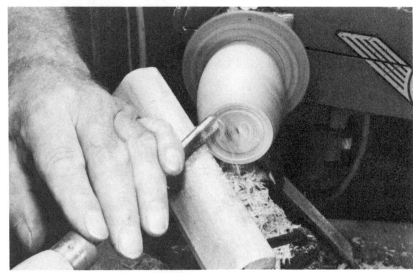

Illus. 60. Hollowing the base with a ³⁄₈-inch (9-mm) high-speed-steel gouge, cutting from a point started with the chisel.

Illus. 61. The box, after the use of the chisel.

32

Illus. 62. Removing the box from the mandrel.

Illus. 63. The finished box, with lid.

Illus. 64. Turned miniature box designs.

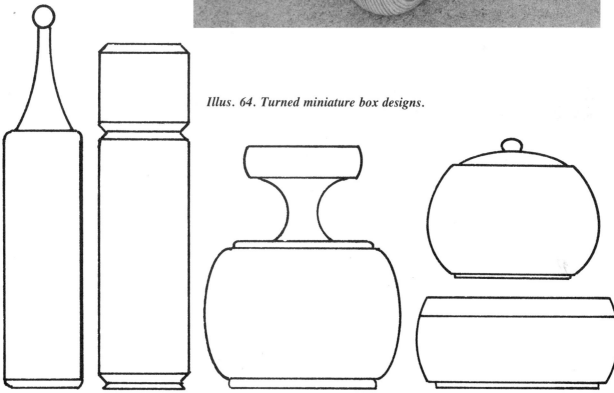

Alternatively, it can be prepared between centers for assembling in a collar chuck. Security is the watchword when turning and boring.

Turn wood between chuck and running center using normal spindle-turning tools. Decide upon the internal diameter of the box, and choose a suitable boring tool. A flatbit is ideal if sawtooth cutters are not available. Cut a rabbet on the box lid the size of the bore. Complete the lid and part off. Bore out the box with the boring tool assembled in the tailstock drill chuck, then clean up (Illus. 65–67). Return the lid to the box, clean up again, and polish the completed box. Part off. Alternatively, cut the inside with a small round-nose gouge.

Illus. 65. Laburnum box held by Coronet small-jaw expanding chuck. Shaping the lid with a ¼-inch (6-mm) gouge.

Illus. 66. Parting off the lid.

Illus. 67. Boring out the body with the sawtooth machine bit.

Using the Precision Chuck

The very latest in woodturning chucks is the precision spigot chuck with screw threads to fit most lathes, marketed by Craft Supplies of Millers Dale, Derbyshire. Among other things, this chuck is ideal for turning miniature boxes. A small spigot is turned on one end of the box. The spigot is gripped by a steel collet, and tightened by a collar. Length of spigot head need not be greater than ⅛-inch (3.17-mm). If turning the spigot is likely to be time-consuming, I will put it on the underside of the box, using a 1½-inch (38.1-mm) plug cutter, and will also cut a recess in the box. This provides the spigot with a depth of ⅛-inch (3.17-mm), and also gives me the ability to use a one-piece turning instead of the manufacturer's suggested two-piece turning (Illus. 68–92).

Illus. 68. Walnut box.

Illus. 69. Exploded spigot chuck, showing spanners and pin chuck.

Illus. 70. Spigot chuck with pre-pared wood block.

Illus. 71. Assembling the wood to the spigot chuck.

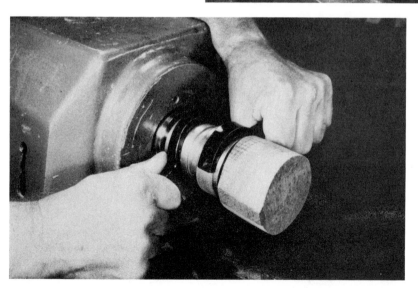

Illus. 72. Tightening the wood in place.

Illus. 73. Roughing the wood to round.

Illus. 74. Planing with the skew chisel.

Illus. 75. Marking out.

Illus. 76. Shaping the lid.

Illus. 77. Lid placed in position for trimming with the skew chisel.

Illus. 78. Parting off the lid.

Illus. 79. Marking out the body with the parting tool.

Illus. 80. Marking out the body with a ¼-inch (6-mm) gouge and boring to depth.

Illus. 81. Beginning to remove waste wood using a ⅜-inch (9-mm) high-speed-steel round-nose gouge.

Illus. 82. Removing waste wood.

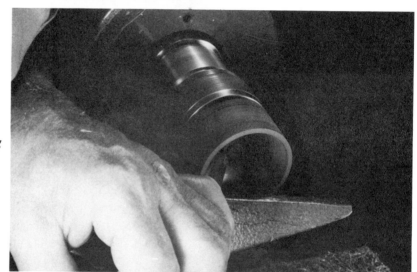

Illus. 83. Gouge approaching final depth.

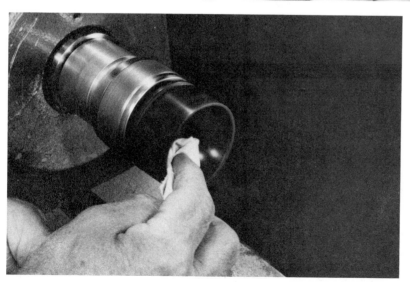

Illus. 84. Polishing the body inside.

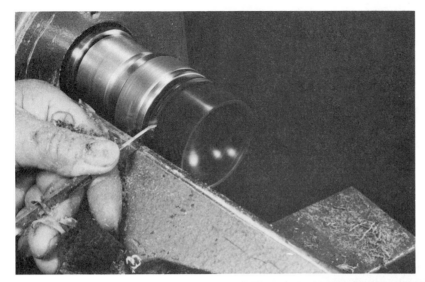

Illus. 85. Parting off the completed body.

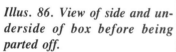

Illus. 86. View of side and underside of box before being parted off.

Illus. 87. Spigot chuck showing waste piece after parting off.

Illus. 88. Making the lid: Wood chuck prepared to receive lid, in order to turn the inside.

Illus. 89. Using the ¼-inch (6-mm) roundnose gouge to shape the inside.

Illus. 90. Shaping.

Illus. 91. Inside finished and polished.

Illus. 92. Completed box, waste piece, and chuck keys.

Illus. 93. Layered box with elm burl lid and rosewood knob.

LAYERED BOXES

Once again, veneers, short ends, and offcuts of wood of every kind can be used to produce extremely useful and beautiful boxes. This project is suggested for the bench, but a lathe may be used instead, with equally satisfying results.

First, select the pieces of wood. Prepare them for size, and plane each face as accurately as possible. (Placing pieces on a band facer will produce a flat surface.) Mark all body pieces in which the middle must be removed. Using the fine blade of the jig saw, carefully cut small holes in those pieces. I use a Hegner saw, which carries out this task perfectly (Illus. 94–98). Clean up each section.

Set up the necessary clamps. Glue up carefully, using a good-quality woodworker's adhesive and aligning each layer. Dry thoroughly overnight. When dry, shape both box and lid with the jig saw or band saw. Clean up with plane and spokeshave, and finish on the band facer. A final finish can be given with fine abrasive paper wrapped around a cork block, or an abrasive board may be used. Polish to a hard finish suitable for constant handling.

Ideally, box interiors should be cut before being glued up so that little work need be done to them afterward. Box interiors can be covered with velvet or other suitable material, particularly when they are to be used for jewelry. Boxes to be used for cigars or cigarettes should be lined with Spanish cedar (*Cedrela Mexicana*), also known as cigar-box cedar.

Illus. 94. The Hegner saw.

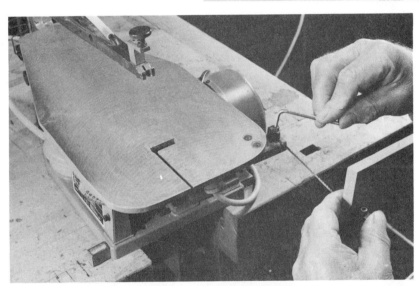

Illus. 95. Setting up the saw blade.

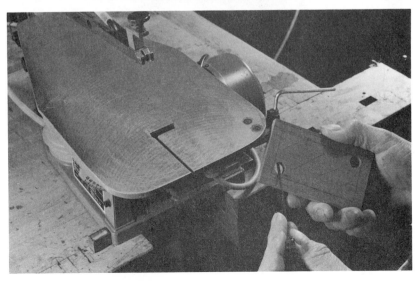

Illus. 96. Inserting the blade through the box section.

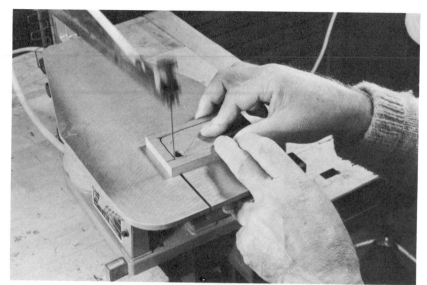

Illus. 97. Cutting the wood.

Illus. 98. Cutting the wood.

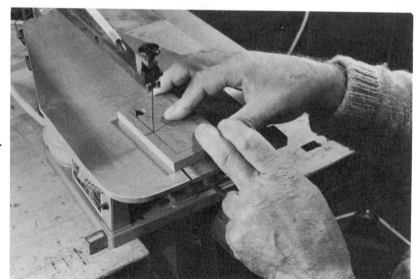

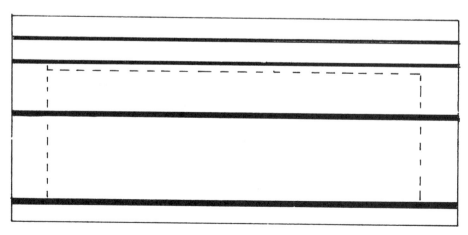

Illus. 99a.

*Illus. 99a-99d. Ideas for single-
and double-thickness veneer
layers.*

Illus. 99b.

Illus. 99c.

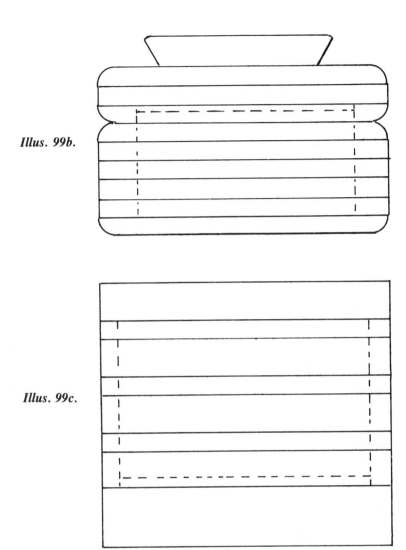

Illus. 99d.

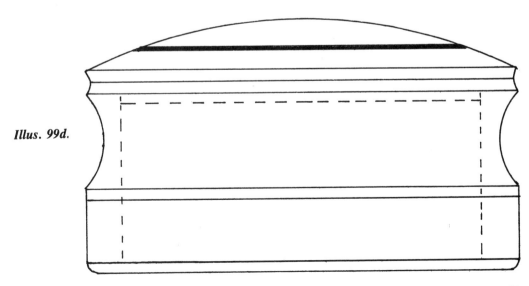

Making the Lid

Make a rebated lid by gluing a piece of wood of the same diameter as the inside of the box to the underside of the lid. This saves machine or hand rebating. Should the lid require a handle, fashion one, by using a sanding machine. The handle can be secured with a glued dowel.

Illus. 100. Layered figured English oak box with ebony handle.

Illus. 101. Layered box in oak with sycamore veneer layer.

Illus. 102. Small cube sculptures of ¾-inch (18-mm) square wood.

CUBE SCULPTURES

The value of using short ends cannot be overemphasized, particularly since this will bring many of the more unusual woods into the work. Pieces of garden trees converted and seasoned at home can also add color and variety.

Cut perfect cubes and bring each one to a fine finish on all sides. Marking out and cutting accurately are vital, thus the tools will need to be sharpened perfectly.

Since the cube will be sculpted by using machine bits in the drill press, a design must be worked out in advance. Each hole must be marked out carefully to produce the desired shape. Hold the block in a vise, exercising extreme caution to avoid scoring or marking the surface. Examine the wood closely, and cut it selectively, aiming for a beautifully strong and thin cube.

Boring Holes

Using the correct boring tool at the proper speed is essential. Forstner bits and sawtooth bits can burn the block if fed too slowly. Using a bit at too fast a rate can cause wood to split, especially if it is thin.

Holes passing through the block completely should be bored from both directions to avoid splintering the outsides. Always place a piece of waste wood beneath the block being bored to protect the boring tool

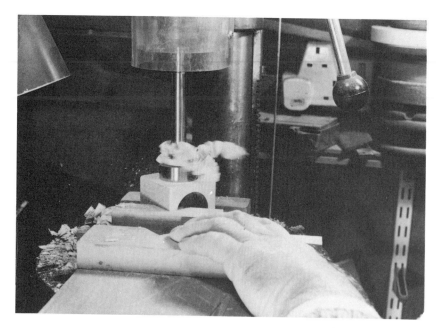

Illus. 103. Boring a cube sculpture on the drill press with a sawtooth cutter.

(Illus. 103). A touch of paraffin (an ordinary candle will do) on the periphery of the bit will ease its passage through the wood.

Finished sculptures can be left unpolished (Illus. 104–105). Painting some surfaces may add depth or create a different appearance altogether. Mount individual cubes on simple bases, or hang them from short lengths of wire. Make multi-cube sculptures by incorporating wood and wire.

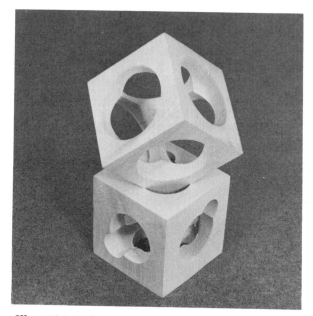

Illus. 104. Cube sculpture.

Illus. 105. Cube sculpture.

Illus. 106. Love spoons in a variety of woods.

LOVE SPOONS

Three hundred years ago, lovesick Welshmen expressed their affection for young maidens by carving them love spoons. The designs incorporated symbols expressing devotion and fidelity. A heart meant love, a wheel implied willingness to work, and eyeglasses showed that the carver needed to see his beloved. Carvers often added chains and cages in spheres, to suggest that their hearts were held captive by love.

Generally, these spoons were cut with simple tools. Most often they were carved in sycamore, beech, or birch, laburnum, holly, or yew. From time to time, fruitwoods were used. Strength was obviously a vital quality, but many a spoon carver chose wood for its color alone.

Everything for the home was made from trees at that time, from furniture to spoons. Probably spoons were made last—after all other needs had been met—from branch wood. Domestic items, particularly kitchen utensils, were classified as *treen*. This is an old English word, meaning "of the trees."

Although my spoons may be carved with a loved one in mind, it would be incorrect to call this work treen. My spoons are rather different, both in design and construction. The enslaved heart is symbolized by a disc inlaid with another disc. The chain is indicated by interlocking circles, which are cut by using a plug cutter as a router bit. The spoon bowl is cut with a carver's hook. (A Welsh version of this

Illus. 107. Love spoons in the making.

Illus. 108. Using a jigsaw to shape the piece.

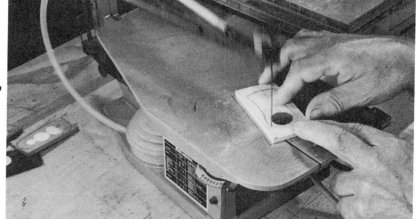

tool has a long handle. One end is held under the carver's arm. The other end is pulled towards the carver. A German version of this tool is very popular.)

I do much of the actual cutting with a jig saw or narrow-blade saw (Illus. 108). For final shaping and finishing, I use a traditional whittling knife or a Swedish-type carver's knife. Various sanding devices, including the flexible-drum sander, complete the spoon.

Illus. 109. Hot-melt glue used to hold the spoon safely during bowl carving. The bench hook is held in the vise.

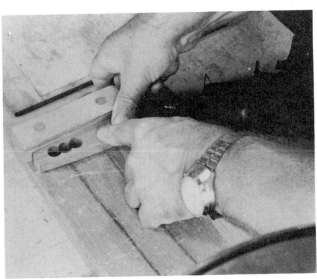

Illus. 110. Pressing the spoon down before the glue sets. When the work is completed it can be lifted safely by placing a thin knife between the spoon and the hook.

Illus. 111. Carving with a small No. 6 gouge.

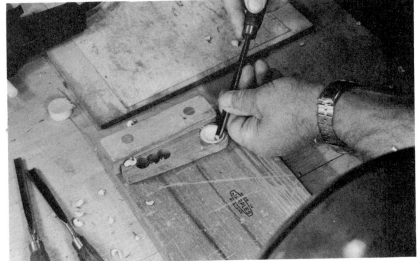

Illus. 112. Finishing the bowl with a No. 6 gouge.

Illus. 113. An alternative method of holding small work: Using the wood hand vise and folding wedges.

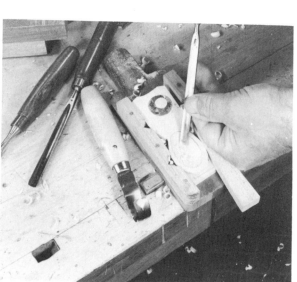

Illus. 114. A second alternative holding method: Using the wood hand vise between bench dogs.

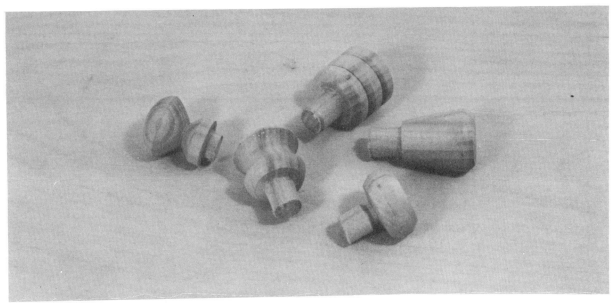

Illus. 115. A variety of knobs.

DOORKNOBS AND HANDLES

Doorknobs and handles are excellent projects for the bench or lathe. Consider making handles for kitchen cabinets, tiny knobs for dressers, even a doorknob for the front door. It is possible to work infinite variations on the bench, but the lathe should be used for purely circular turning only.

On the Lathe

Attach a piece of waste softwood to a faceplate. Using a hot-melt glue gun, glue onto it a selected piece of hardwood. Turn the face of the job, to shape it. Bore a hole in the handle with a tiny drill assembled in the tailstock chuck. This hole will be used for re-centering when the block is reversed. Polish and finish.

Remove the wood from the glue chuck with a knife. Reglue it, and quickly attach it to the chuck, using the tailstock running center to make sure that the block is centered. Place the drill chuck in the tailstock. Fit sawtooth cutters, and bore 2¼-inch (5.71-cm) holes successively to a depth of ⅛-inch (3.17-mm), 2-inch (5.08-cm) holes to ⅜-inch (9.52-mm), and 1½-inch (3.81-cm) holes completely through the wood and into the glue-chuck block itself. This will protect the wood from splintering at the back of the hole. In the absence of sawtooth cutters, use a parting tool and gouge to do the boring.

55

Illus. 116. Making door and drawer pulls: The blank is as-sembled to the glue chuck using the hot-melt glue gun.

Illus. 117. The blank is turned and drilled with a small drill. The hole is used for reverse as-sembly, with the tailstock dead center.

Illus. 118. Breaking the glue joint with a knife to separate it from the glue chuck.

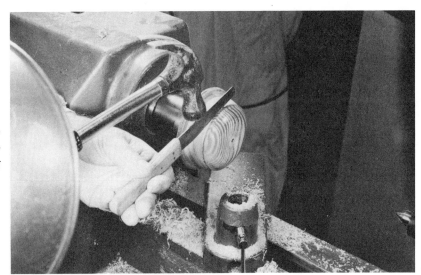

Illus. 119. The door pull reversed, centered with the tailstock center, and glued, using the hot-melt glue gun.

Illus. 120. Boring the finger recess.

Illus. 121. The second boring.

Illus. 122. The final bore, completely through the work.

Illus. 123. Door or drawer handle of pitch pine turned on the lathe.

Remove wood from block. Cut a 2¼-inch (5.71-cm) wide plastic laminate disc, and glue it into the recess. The job is now complete. Sawing the wood in half will result in two handles.

Illus. 124. Making a door handle: A block of imbuia is mounted on the screw chuck.

Illus. 125. Shaping the block with the roundnose gouge.

Illus. 126. Shaping.

Illus. 127. Shaping.

Illus. 128. Shaping.

Illus. 129. Cutting the finger recess in the back.

Illus. 130. Boring a hole with the sawtooth cutter for the center plug.

Illus. 131. Gluing the plug, with the tailstock quill pushing the plug in.

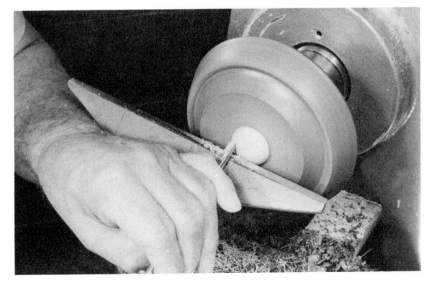

Illus. 132. Turning the center plug.

Illus. 133. The completed door handle in imbuia with a syca-more handle.

Illus. 134. Some ideas for door handles to turn on the lathe.

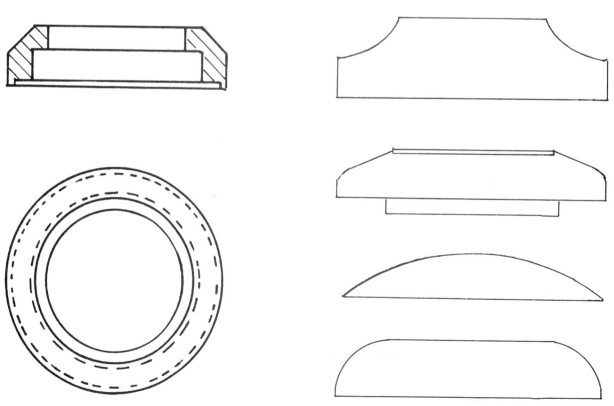

Illus. 135. Making drawer pulls and small door knobs: Material is assembled between a cone center and a running center.

Illus. 136. Roughing out with a ³/₄-inch (18-mm)-deep standard gouge.

Illus. 137. Planing with a skew chisel.

Illus. 138. Marking out pieces.

Illus. 139. Marking out pieces with a parting tool.

Illus. 140. Shaping the pieces with a chisel.

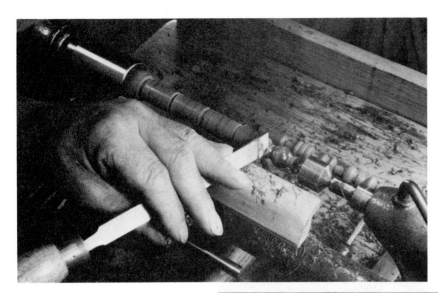

Illus. 141. More shaping.

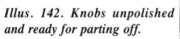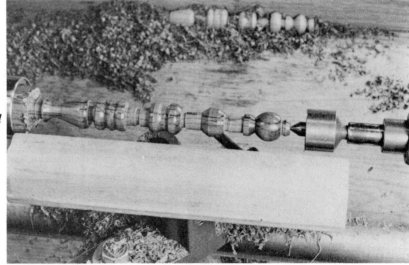

Illus. 142. Knobs unpolished and ready for parting off.

Illus. 143. Various knobs.

At the Bench

Virtually any shape is possible at the bench. Use ring-saw-type cutters, Forstner bits, or sawtooth cutters mounted in the machine drill press to cut the holes (Illus. 144–145). The disc inserted in the back of the handles can range from a laminated one for kitchen furniture to an exotic veneer matching or contrasting with other pieces for other furniture. To finish, paint or polish handles, or oil and wax them.

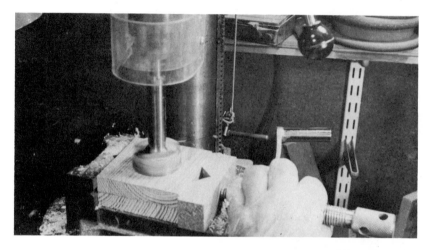

Illus. 144. Making door and drawer pulls: Initial boring with a Forstner bit.

Illus. 145. Second boring.

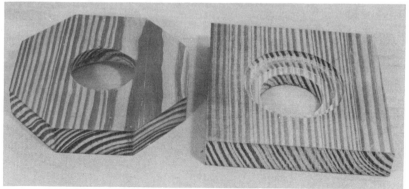

Illus. 146. Door and drawer handles in pitch pine bored on the drill press.

GEARSTICK AND WALKING STICK KNOBS

Illus. 147. Gear lever knob in rosewood. Gear positions marked with steel balls.

The average automobile has many showy plastic parts. More expensive autos often seem much more luxurious because finely selected exotic veneers are used instead of plastic. Frequently, these are complemented by the addition of a well-turned gear-lever knob. Turning such a knob is not difficult for the average woodturner. Wood is mounted on the screw chuck and turned in the usual fashion. Gear positions are indicated with various types of inlay. Contrasting wood is the simplest to use, but other materials can be considered. If an exotic wood is used with lines of silver inlay or spots of silver wire, it will produce a Rolls Royce job.

Making the Gearstick

Before inlaying, turn the knob to shape and almost to size (Illus. 148–151). Not all hands are the same size, so fit the handle to the hand. Do not remove the knob from the screw chuck, but remove the whole assembly from the lathe. Bore out holes, or cut grooves for the inlay. Glue the inlay in place. Use P.V.A. glue for wood, and epoxy-resin glue for other materials, such as metal, glass, and jewels. When the glue is completely dry, return the work to the lathe and carefully remove the surplus inlay, using fine sandpaper (glass paper). Finally, use a hard finish for the polish. Detach the completed work from the screw chuck.

Illus. 148. Making the gear-lever knob: Rosewood block is bored and ready to screw into the wood screw chuck.

Illus. 149. Roughing the wood with a ¾-inch (18-mm) standard deep gouge.

Illus. 150. Planing the block with a chisel.

Illus. 151. Planing the top with the gouge.

Remove the plastic gear knob from the auto. If possible, remove the nut by which it is attached to the lever. If this cannot be done, obtain a duplicate nut and cut a recess in the underside of the knob for it. Glue it in place with epoxy resin. When handling the knob, wrap it carefully in a piece of soft, protective material, to avoid glue damage, vise marks, or even fingerprints. Fit the knob onto the lever and drive away, the neighbors looking on enviously.

Walking Stick Knobs

These knobs can be quite plain, the grain and color of the wood determining their beauty, or they can be inlaid. (Refer to *Costume Jewelry*, page 13, for details on inlaying.) Hardwood knobs can often be unpolished; constant handling will provide the polish.

Some years ago I was presented with a Malacca cane fitted with silver mounts. When it was new it must have cost a great deal, but unfortunately the knob handle was gone. I was determined to return the walking stick to its pristine glory, and I did so, with a piece of lignum vitae that matched the Malacca. I again used a screw chuck to attach the wood to the lathe. Had I had a pin chuck, I would have chosen the ½-inch (12.7-mm) size and pre-bored the wood, using a ½-inch (12.7-mm) sawtooth machine bit. With a pin chuck, it is possible to remove a job for further bench work and subsequently return it to the chuck in exactly the same position.

You may not have Malacca cane, but a number of others can be substituted. Canes may be turned on the lathe, but I prefer hunting in the hedgerow for a long, straight branch.

Illus. 152. Making the walking stick knob: The wood block is mounted to the screw chuck and turned to shape with the ³⁄₈-inch (9-mm) gouge.

Illus. 153. Shaping with the gouge.

Illus. 154. Setting up to bore with sawtooth machine bit.

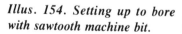

Illus. 155. Using the sawtooth machine bit to bore a plug insert.

Illus. 156. Gluing in the plug.

Illus. 157. Using the tailstock to push home the plug.

Illus. 158. Inserting a smaller plug after the assembly has been removed from the lathe and the hole bored on the drill press.

Illus. 159. Turning the inserted plug.

Illus. 160. The finished walking stick knob is bubinga inlaid with plugs of sycamore and bog oak.

Honiton bobbin

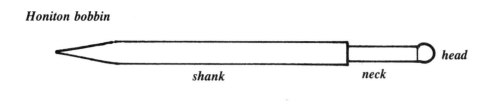

shank   neck   head

East Midlands bobbin

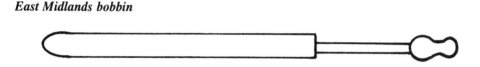

Illus. 161. Lace bobbins.

LACE BOBBINS

Wonderful revivals are taking place in crafts, not the least among them the revival of hand lacemaking. Lace guilds and societies are springing up everywhere. There are two main types of lace: bobbin lace, in which the thread is plaited and woven, and needlepoint lace, which is sewed with a needle and thread.

Bobbin lace requires a bobbin at the end of each length of thread. Each piece of lace may require up to thirty pairs of bobbins. Thus, purchasing bobbins can present a formidable cash problem.

A glance at a lacemaker's pairs will indicate the delightful variety of bobbin shapes, and also the wide range of woods used. Bobbinmaking will instantly appeal to woodturners, particularly ones who save every bit of wood for the day (which sometimes never seems to arrive) when a project arises needing such trifles.

Bobbin Functions

You must understand the use of the lace bobbin to appreciate that although there seems to be an infinite number of bobbin shapes, there are certain basic requirements they must all fulfill. First, the bobbin is used to weave with, the little shank acting as a handle. Second, by its weight a bobbin holds the thread taut, so be careful to judge the final weight of each bobbin to ensure even tension. Third, a bobbin stores thread and permits it to be fed to the work when needed.

Bobbin style depends largely on the area the lace comes from. There are many styles in Europe. In the United Kingdom the best-known lace style is that of Honiton, in glorious Devon. This is extremely fine lace, requiring a pointed bobbin, almost needlelike in its fineness. Bedfordshire or East Midland bobbins are very thin. Unlike Honiton, they have parallel sides.

Bobbins are sometimes also seen with a spangle. A spangle consists of glass beads attached through a tiny hole drilled in the bobbin. Bedfordshire bobbins have nine bead spangles.

Making Bobbins

The basic requirement for the lathe is a means of driving these small pairs. I used to use a small attachment tapered to fit into the headstock of the lathe. I cut a pyramid-shaped hole at one end for small round- or square-sectioned wood to fit into. (The normal driving fork of the lathe is quite inadequate for this work, being far too large.) Driving cones are now available for both head and tailstock. These can be screwed to the lathe headstock or fitted to a Morse-taper adaptor to fit any lathe. The cones for the tailstock attach to the running center, and can also be obtained with number one, two, or three morse tapers.

Wood must be selected very carefully. The finished bobbins must be slender; therefore, the grain should be long, straight, and without knots or flaws. The wood must be free from oil, resin, or other matter that could cause damage to the thread.

Begin by cutting square blocks. Leave enough wood to allow for waste in the chuck or cones (Illus. 162–163). Make a cardboard template to check if the sizes are accurate. If there are not too many shapes intended, this could be cut from thin sheet aluminum. Alternatively, a needle-type profile gauge could be used.

Illus. 162. Making lace bobbins: A blank is mounted between a mandrel in the headstock with a small square hole for driving and a small running center in the tailstock.

Illus. 163. Turned wood.

Most of the turning is done with a skew chisel. Support the wood while cutting it, due to its thinness. I usually keep the fingers of my left hand over the top of my work, supporting the chisel with my thumb (Illus. 164). Some turners prefer to bring their fingers under the tool rest, holding their work from behind. I find this rather awkward. Choose a method that is both comfortable and safe.

Illus. 164. Planing with the skew chisel using the fingers of the left hand over the top of the work to support the thin turning.

Do not press down too heavily, or the wood may begin to burn. Use the lathe at top speed, sharpen the chisel like a razor, and give the bevel a good polishing. Doing so will remove the need for sanding in the finishing stages. Roughing down can be done with a ⅜-inch (9.52-mm) gouge or a ¼-inch (6.35-mm) one. The ¼-inch (6.35-mm) beading

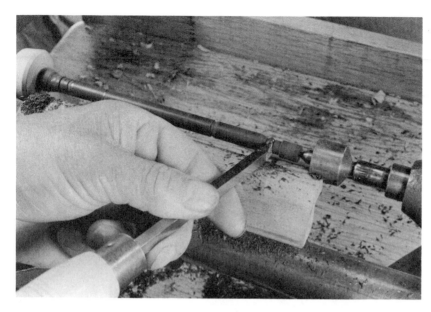

Illus. 165. Beading with a skew chisel.

chisel can be used for planing and shaping (Illus. 165). The final finish must be extremely smooth, and the thread must not catch in the bobbin. Sand with a fine-grit paper only if a satiny finish has not been achieved with the tools. Do not apply any polish. Traditionally, bobbins were used straight from the machine.

Turn down to the main diameter with a chisel. Use the template to mark out, scoring very lightly with the long corner of the skew chisel to transfer each measurement. Cut and shape the long shank and then the neck, cutting the shoulders very carefully with the long corner of the chisel (Illus. 166–168). Shape the head as in beading. Carefully sand if necessary, and part off with the skew chisel, cutting down equally at both ends almost to the last fibre. Often a bobbin will break through but still run on the waste.

Illus. 166. Squaring with the skew chisel.

Illus. 167. Using the heel of the chisel to square into the corner.

Illus. 168. Tapering with the skew chisel.

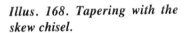

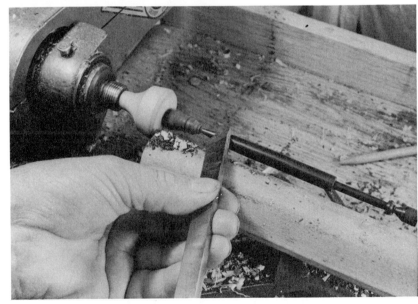

There is no better way for the beginner to learn the art of spindle turning than by using a chisel to make bobbins. Tools must be sharp (no sharpening on the fast-moving double-ended grinder here), and they must be applied correctly, with the bevel rubbing. The very thinness of the work prevents weight and brute strength from being applied.

Illus. 169. Various table mats.

TABLE MATS WITH THE ROUTER

Table-mat design depends on the shape of the router bit. Since the mat is worked on both sides, each cut breaks through into the cuts on the reverse side, and an attractive and regular pattern is created. Choice of wood is vital. It must be long, straight-grained, free of knots, and able to resist heat, cold, and moisture.

The router can be hand-held, with repeated settings of the fence, but if a router stand is available, it is much easier to pass the wood over the router. This method also makes it unnecessary to fix the wood on the bench before each cut.

Method

First prepare the wood, accurately planing to size and shape, finishing the edges so that they are ready for polishing. Draw the position of each cut exactly, and set the router so that the breakthrough on the reverse side will create the desired shape.

It is a good idea to do a dummy cut first. Set the fence for the first cut inside the edge, then do the cuts on both sides and on all four edges (Illus. 170 and 172). When this is completed, re-set the fence and make eight passes, as before. Obviously, the number of passes will depend upon the design.

Illus. 170 (right). Cutting the mats with the router assembled to a stand.

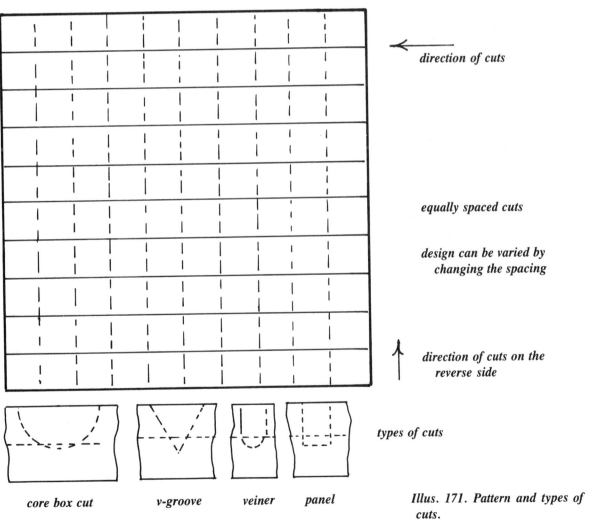

direction of cuts

equally spaced cuts

design can be varied by changing the spacing

direction of cuts on the reverse side

types of cuts

core box cut   v-groove   veiner   panel

Illus. 171. Pattern and types of cuts.

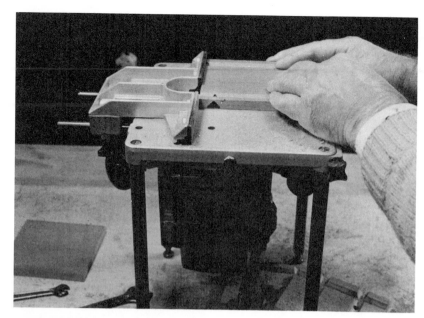

Illus. 172. Cutting the table mat with the work turned over.

Illus. 173. Completed table mat.

When the router work is completed, use very fine sandpaper (glass paper) to clean up. If the router bit is finely sharpened, sanding may not be necessary. Choose a polish that is both moisture- and heat-resistant. A wood like teak will not require a finish.

Be prepared to make a fairly simple design, if only for the sake of the person who has to clean the table mats and keep them in good shape.

Illus. 174. Box in English yew with plugs in lid of rosewood and plugs in box of laburnum.

TURNED WORK WITH INLAID PLUGS

Turned work can be decorated with plugs of contrasting woods. Plugs may be cut with a plug cutter as previously described. (See page 15). Boring holes for plugs poses a few problems, however. The job is best done on a lathe, since a lathe gives a high degree of accuracy and allows the block to remain where it is.

I used to use a Myford ML8 lathe for this task, the locking holes drilled in the headstock pulley functioning as a dividing head (Illus. 175). Since I no longer have this lathe in my workshop, I have adopted a system that can work on any lathe.

I was fortunate to have a large aluminum faceplate that could be screwed to the lefthand end of my Varispeed lathe (Illus. 176–177). I drilled holes into it big enough to receive a spring-loaded plunger. I constructed a small bracket of mild steel strip and fitted it with a small plunger. I screwed the plunger assembly to the middle of the top of the headstock casing. This provided a dividing head that gave me a variety of boring positions and also locked the work in place securely.

In place of the tee rest, I put my Wolf drill-stand pillar and drill, complete with ½-inch (12.7-mm) capacity chuck (Illus. 178). Fitted with sawtooth machine cutters (multi-spur), this can be used to bore side holes.

Illus. 175. Drill assembly for inlaying plugs: This is the earlier version, for the Myford ML8 lathe. The locking device using holes in the pulley serves as the dividing head. The stand is mounted in place of the tool rest.

Illus. 176 (left). Boring assembly for the lathe: The dividing head is made from a large face-plate.

Illus. 177 (below). Spring plunger device for locking the dividing head screwed to the top of the lathe headstock.

Illus. 178. Wolf drill stand fitted in place of a tee rest.

Making holes in the face of a bowl requires a further attachment. The drill-stand pillar must be removed, and one with a 90° bend substituted. I made one from steel rod. Mount the drill assembly horizontally, and bore holes in the face of the work. Use a drill press or an electric drill mounted in a stand to bore plugs. It is dangerous to use plug cutters in a hand-held electric drill. Alternatively, plugs can be cut from spindles turned on the lathe. I prefer to have the grain running in the same direction as the turned wood, which precludes the use of plugs from turned spindles.

Illus. 179. Bent bar used to turn the drill horizontally.

Illus. 180. Indian rosewood bowl with inlaid Welsh holly plugs.

Turning a Bowl with Edge-Decorated Plugs

Choose woods of contrasting colors, after determining the function of the bowl. Attach the basic block to a faceplate and turn the underside. Leave a recess for an expanding collet chuck, so that the work can be re-mounted. Bring to a perfect finish and polish as needed.

Remove the faceplate, and screw in the expanding chuck. Remount to the lathe. Remove the tee rest, and set up the bent pillar with the drill placed horizontally. Be sure that the body lies vertically and is securely clamped before beginning to drill. Bore out each hole using the dividing head to position each hole correctly.

Carefully glue in the plugs. If necessary, remove the bowl from the lathe to do this. Push each plug into the bottom of the hole. Do not place too much glue in the holes. When dry, turn to shape, and complete the bowl.

Turning a Bowl with Plugs on the Face and Edges

Assemble a bowl and turn as before, but this time leave a fairly wide flat face for the plugs. With the assembly set up for boring face holes, bore a series of holes quite near the edge. Insert plugs as before, and leave the glue to dry. When turning, be careful not to cut back the plugs so that the bottom of the hole shows. If this happens, there may be a nasty gap caused by the brad point of the sawtooth cutter.

Many variations are possible, but avoid overdecorating. Choose only woods that contrast appealingly, and try to choose them of equal hardness, for a better, more even surface.

Turning a Deep Bowl with Plugs Inserted into Plugs

Turn the bowl as before. When the first plugs are glued and set, bore a smaller hole into each plug, for a contrasting plug. When the glue is set, the bowl can be turned and completed.

Illus. 181. Small finials.

FINIALS AND HALF AND QUARTER TURNINGS

Finials present a simple exercise in spindle turning—that is, in actually cutting wood to shape. There is a problem with driving material, though, particularly if the finials are very tiny. A small mandrel with a pyramid-shaped hole in the headstock is the simplest solution. Anyone fortunate enough to have a number of Coronet cones will not have any difficulty making finials.

Always prepare a template if several finials are required. Choose the wood carefully. Ideally, it should be long and strong but not brittle, to give sharp corners and an excellent finish without using sandpaper (glass paper).

Cut several squares long enough to allow for waste in the cones or mandrel. Mount and turn down almost to size with a small roughing tool (Illus. 183). Mark out from the template, then use the skew chisel to cut beads, tapers, and slow curves (Illus. 184–187). Use a ¼-inch round-nose gouge to cut coves or similar shapes (Illus. 188). Keep the bevel "looking" at the wood and the polished bevel and sharp edge will do the rest. Finish by machine, if possible (Illus. 190). Very large finials for buildings can also be turned this way. Use larger cones or a normal driving fork and running centers.

Illus. 182. Turning a finial: Block is mounted between a cone screwed to the headstock and a running center in the tailstock.

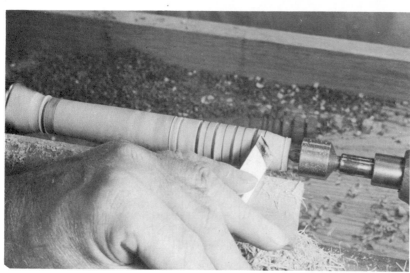

Illus. 183. Shaping with the chisel.

Illus. 184. Shaping with the chisel.

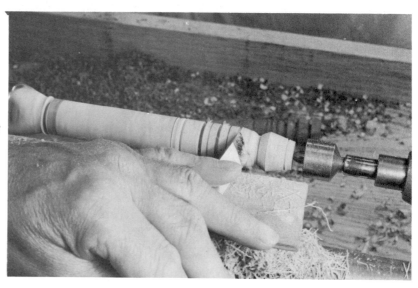

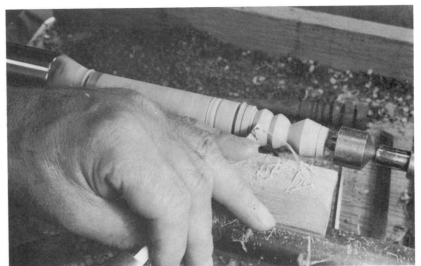

Illus. 185. Shaping with the chisel.

Illus. 186. Shaping with the chisel.

Illus. 187. Squaring down with the chisel.

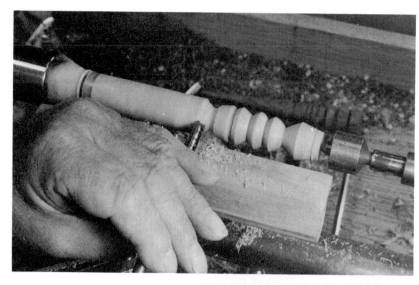

Illus. 188. Coving with the roundnose gouge.

Illus. 189. Tapering with the skew chisel.

Illus. 190. Polishing with the shavings.

Illus. 191. Finial ready for parting off.

Quarter Turnings

I used to make these by gluing four perfect squares, using glue and brown paper. I later graduated to the hot-melt glue gun. This enabled me to use wood immediately, and the wood came apart easily after the turning was completed. Either of these methods can be used with wood mounted between a fork and running center. With the introduction of cone centers, one at the headstock and another attached to the running center at the tailstock end, the need for glue has been eliminated.

Prepare squares of the desired length, allowing for waste. Place four together, insert into the cones and tighten on the tailstock. Turn to completion, and remove four perfect quarter turnings from the lathe. If more are needed, place one completed turning and three blanks in the cones. Turn, using the completed quarter as the master. Place a sheet of white paper at the back of the lathe, to assist in sighting the profile as the lathe spins. Half turnings can also be done using the cones. See pages 92–98 for further details on quarter turnings.

Illus. 192. Dice in boxwood with sawdust spots.

DICE

Dice can be functional or purely decorative. If they are to be functional, they will require extremely accurate cutting of very carefully selected wood. The wood must withstand wear and tear, be the right weight, and have an attractive long, straight grain. Welsh holly, extremely white in color, has all the necessary qualities.

Plane and saw each side very carefully, so that the dice are extremely accurate and very smooth even before being sanded. Do the final sanding with an abrasive board to which has been glued the finest sandpaper (glass paper) available.

Mark the dice, using tiny wood plugs or dowels. Aluminum, brass, or even silver make attractive choices for cubes made of dark wood. Alternatively, plastic rod or epoxy-resin mixtures are other options. It is difficult to bore and inlay into very small dice. Another method is to bore very shallow holes with a drill and then use paint to mark the dice.

Boring

Marking out and boring must be done with great accuracy and considerable care. If ordinary drills or wood drills will be used, mark each position with a punch, to ensure accurate placement of the drill. Use a spur-point drill, if possible. Stop the drill before boring each hole and carefully reset the work. Bore deeply enough to hold the inset wire securely. Do not bore too deeply, or the weight of the metal will upset the accurate functioning of the dice. Glue in place with epoxy-resin glue, and sand carefully. Complete with a matte polish. Normal-sized dice can be kept safely in a box made up as a die. The dice pictured were made of hardwoods (Illus. 122–124). Some of the spots are ball bearings.

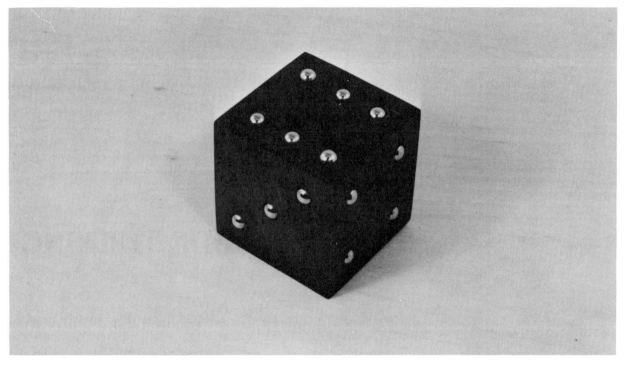

Illus. 193. Dice in partridge with steel ball bearings for spots.

Illus. 194. Dice in bubinga with steel ball bearings for spots.

Illus. 195. Inside/outside turned candlestick in mahogany.

INSIDE/OUTSIDE TURNING

Cone drives, a relatively new addition to the shop, greatly simplify turning (Illus. 196). At the same time, they offer new challenges to the woodworker's ingenuity. Using cone centers it is possible to set up and turn square, round, and odd-shaped sections without preparation and without driving forks or running centers. Using cones also allows completed pieces to be returned to the lathe for re-cutting or correction.

Illus. 196. Inside/outside turning cones with arbors to suit the lathe.

Perhaps the best feature is that four square sections can be set up, held securely, and turned at one time. Once turned, they can be moved, their positions reversed, and the turning continued. Hence the term "inside/outside turning." First the insides will be turned on the outside, then their positions reversed, and the outsides turned. This is a complicated statement, but a simple operation, as the photographs show.

Turning a Lamp

Select a length of wood, and plane it square. Cut the wood into four equal lengths, and place them in matching cones set in the headstock and tailstock of the lathe (Illus. 197–198). Using a chisel and gouge, turn

Illus. 197. Cones mounted in the lathe.

Illus. 198. Wood quarters in place.

to size and shape (Illus. 199–200). It is best to make an accurate drawing before turning, and to check the size and shape throughout the cutting.

Complete the first stage of the turning, and polish. Remove the four pieces from the cones. Reverse positions, so that the turned faces are on the inside. Glue together. When dry, again place between cones (Illus. 201). Turn as before, keeping an eye on the drawing, and checking constantly for size (Illus. 202–203). Remove the turnings from the cones. Remove the tailstock cone, and carefully bore a hole with a hole-boring drill. Prepare the material and turn a base. Assemble the work, clean, and hand polish.

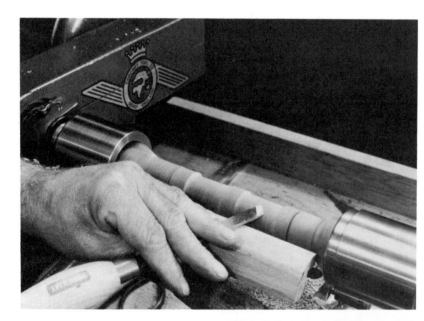

Illus. 199. Roughing down with ¾-inch (18-mm)-deep standard gouge.

Illus. 200. Shaping the inside with a skew chisel.

Illus. 201. Four quarters reversed, glued, and reassembled to the lathe.

Illus. 202. Turning almost completed. Note the sharp image as the lathe spins.

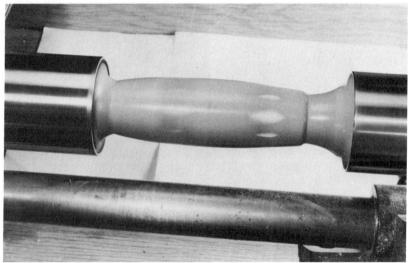

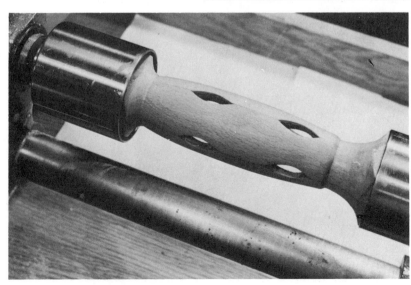

Illus. 203. Completed turning.

Illus. 204. Inside/outside turn-ing with cone centers: Four square pieces placed between the cone centers.

Illus. 205. Roughing with the ¾-inch (18-mm)-deep gouge.

Illus. 206. Planing with the skew chisel.

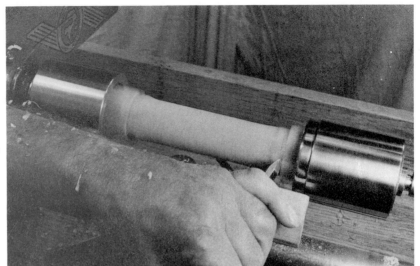

Illus. 207. Squaring the ends.

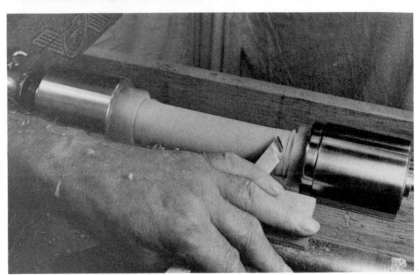

Illus. 208. Using the heel of the chisel to finish.

Illus. 209. Pieces shaped and ready to turn inside.

97

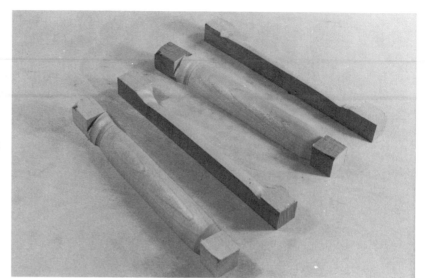

Illus. 210. Pieces removed from the cones.

Illus. 211. Pieces reassembled inside out.

Illus. 212. Roughing the pieces to shape. Note the image shown by the slots as the lathe turns.

Illus. 213. Taking a look while the lathe is off.

Illus. 214. Pieces in their final shape.

Illus. 215. Inside/outside turned pieces before the final gluing. Note their oval sections.

Illus. 216. Clock case in maple.

CLOCK CASES ON THE BENCH OR LATHE

Battery-operated clock movements are now readily available with a wide variety of hands. Design variations are almost infinite. The designs pictured here require only the lathe and one or two types of bench activity.

Spindles on most movements are generally only ⅝ inch (16 mm) long. Know the length of the spindle before making a design, since it will determine the final thickness of the middle of the clock face. The thickness of the clock body determines the size of the finished clock case.

On the Lathe

The method of attaching the block to the lathe depends partly on the design. If only the face will be shaped and the numerals put on separately, use a wood chuck. The back of the clock can then be cut with turning tools. Attach the material to the faceplate and turn it to fit the chuck.

Turn small clock cases by attaching the block to the screw chuck, turning the face, and then reversing the block to cut the movement recess. The middle hole will have to be bored, using a boring tool in the drill press.

Illus. 217. Making a clock case in sycamore: Preparing the block for mounting to the screw chuck. The center hole is cleared with the roundnose gouge.

Illus. 218. The blank and chuck ready for assembly.

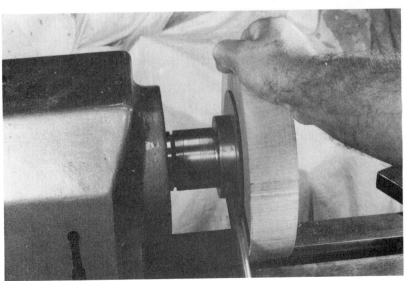

Illus. 219. Mounting the blank using a steel pin to hold the chuck.

Illus. 220. Mounted blank and selected gouge. Note the round nose—Stockdale's own.

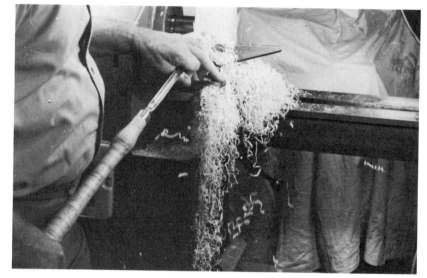

Illus. 221. Turning to round.

Illus. 222. Turning the recess in the back to receive the clock mechanism. Note the Super Flute gouge.

Illus. 223. Turning continuing.

Illus. 224. Turning continuing.

Illus. 225. Squaring the inside with the gouge.

Illus. 226. Flattening the back. Moving to the right.

Illus. 227. Flattening the back. Moving to the left.

Illus. 228. Cutting a small chamfer on the back edge.

Plugs can be used instead of numerals to mark the face. Bore the holes by using a lathe and the dividing-head unit. Accuracy is crucial. Holes can also be marked out with a compass and ruler and bored with a drill press. Another variation can be created by inserting plugs into the edge and then turning the face, revealing the side of each plug. These appear as narrow parallel or tapered bars. Plugs inserted near the edge can be cut away partially, to mark the hour with segments of endgrain.

Illus. 229. Block bored to receive black walnut plugs.

Illus. 230. Facing with the gouge.

Illus. 231. Facing and shaping.

Illus. 232. Facing and shaping.

Illus. 233. Finishing with the gouge.

Illus. 234. Polishing.

Illus. 235. Finished clock case.

Illus. 236. Clock case in fiddleback sycamore with American black walnut plugs.

On the Bench

Designs can incorporate both straight and curved lines, and can be cut from solid blocks or made up of strip wood. At the outset, note the size of the clock movement and the spindle. Use a band saw, jigsaw, bow saw, or coping saw to cut curves. Finish with a plane, spokeshave, or compass plane. Work straight edges with a plane and saw.

Mark hours by inlaying strips, squares, or rounds. Cut strips with a fine chisel, squares with a hollow square mortise chisel and bit, and rounds with a sawtooth machine bit, Forstner bit, or flatbit held in the drill press. For inlays, use contrasting woods, metals such as copper, brass, or aluminum, plastics, or wet mixes of epoxy-resin glue and tinted sawdust.

Illus. 237. A variety of plastic and ceramic clock faces.

Consider round or square ceramic tile and plastic faces as well (Illus. 237). Tiles are ideal for woodturners. Square tiles lend themselves to frame construction (Illus. 238). Tiles can be mounted on baseboards covered by a variety of materials: colored burlap (hessian), plastic laminates, veneers, mirrors, leather, and synthetic fibres used in the furniture trade.

Finally, keep in mind the design possibilities inherent in pendulum movements, and try to take advantage of them.

Illus. 238. Clock case with deep framing. Burlap (hessian)-covered background for specially designed ceramic tiles.

Illus. 239. Barometer in walnut.

APPENDICES

APPENDIX A

ENAMELLING

Simple enamelling needs very little equipment other than a torch, a tripod, and a piece of gauze. But a more serious involvement, or one including an excursion into silver work, will call for additional equipment. Certainly, anything complicated will require a kiln. Many craftspeople live outside the city, in areas where services like gas and electricity are not readily available. So, when examining kilns, choose one that can be used anywhere.

I use a gas-fired kiln (Illus. 240). It reaches a 1900-degree F. (900-degree C.) maximum in ten minutes. It is simple to light, since it ignites using a piezo spark. A heat-control valve offers simple temperature control. The door allows for easy view and permits fumes to exit. When fully opened, it clears the chamber, to give full access to the contents inside. Using a small, covered crucible, I can melt gold or silver in this kiln. This enables me to do cuttlebone and other casting. This kiln has a removable burner and refractory tile. It operates on natural gas, propane, or butane. The latter two are readily available in canisters and pressurized containers.

A smaller kiln is ideal for anyone who intends to work in enamel only. Choose a kiln designed to work off natural or bottled gas, preferably one that uses disposable cartridges of butane. Heat input will enable the kiln to be used for scrolling and other enamel work without a significant temperature drop when the door is opened.

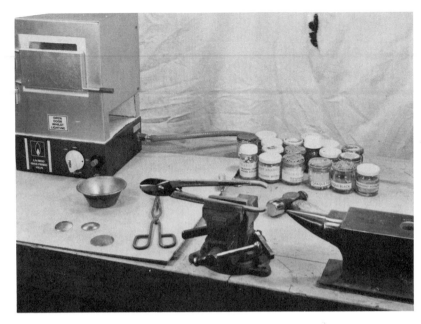

Illus. 240. An enameller's bench all set up. Note the asbestos sheet under the kiln.

For soldering small silver pieces, cloisonné, and other jewelry work, a torch is necessary. I have a very good one, with an electrically driven air pump. It produces a precisely controlled needlepoint flame suitable for small pieces. The torch can be hand-held, or attached to a base and used at 30°, 60°, or 90° angles. It can be used with natural gas, but I prefer disposable cartridges. There is a fixed pressure regulator with a control valve, and a stand to hold the butane cartridge. (See pages 141–145, Hardening Treatment of Woodworking Tools.)

Sometimes I require a heavier flame, and my regular torch is inadequate. I use an air blower and either natural or propane gas. Some air blowers must be equipped with a valve and gauge, so be careful to use the correct type and size nose. This equipment is not overly expensive, and the person who has it is set for life.

Basic Enamelling

Simple enamelling is best done on copper or gilding metal. First cut the metal, then anneal and clean. To anneal metal, heat to a pale red color, then immerse in 1/10 solution of sulphuric acid. Wash thoroughly. Next, clean enamel by washing until the water runs clear and tiny particles no longer rise to the surface. Coarse enamel may need grinding with a mortar and pestle. Always dry enamel before use, and store in airtight jars.

Coat copper with a solution of gum tragacanth before applying enamel. To prepare solution, first mix gum with enough methylated spirits to form a paste, then combine ¼ ounce paste and one pint water. Store in an airtight container in a cool place, and mixture should have an indefinite lifespan.

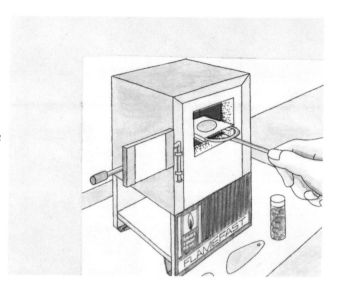

Illus. 241. Lifting work into the kiln with a fork.

Apply enamel by using a tiny sieve and tapping onto coated metal. Using a trivet to support the metal, place in a preheated kiln (Illus. 241). Alternatively, apply heat to the back of the metal with a torch. Two to three minutes should suffice.

Most work requires counter-enamelling. This is a coating of enamel on the back of the work. Counter-enamelling makes for stronger work, by countering the curving and metal distortion that occurs due to heating, and minimizes the likelihood of cracks or chips in the finished work, by balancing the weight on both sides of the metal. It is essential to counter-enamel when several firings are needed and metal distortion is a real danger. Large pieces almost invariably need counter-enamelling. It is not crucial with smaller pieces, and the metal can be slightly convex or concave, depending on the type of work.

Should the enamel be applied too thinly, the copper will not be sealed off from the air. Small indents in the enamel will result. To solve this problem, coat the metal with gum tragacanth again, add additional enamel, and fire once more. If enamel is applied too heavily, it will crawl or pile up. This can be repaired by further firings to level the surface. Be careful not to overload metal. Enamel should never be thicker than the metal it rests on. Slightly underfire when several coats of enamel are required.

Scrolling

Scrolling is a technique using lump enamel placed randomly or in a carefully conceived pattern on a piece of metal, and using a scrolling tool to create a pattern as the lumps melt and form a pool of color (Illus. 242).

Counter-enamel the back. Then turn the metal over, apply gum tragacanth, and dust on a thin layer of enamel. Apply the lump enamel. Return the work to the kiln. As the lumps melt, place the point of one scrolling tool on the metal to hold it in place, and use another for the

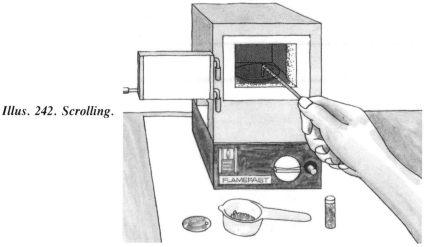

Illus. 242. Scrolling.

actual scrolling. Drawing the point through a lump will elongate it and cause it to float along the enamel. Many designs are possible. Just be careful not to overload the metal with too much enamel, and do not overfire.

Cloisonné Enamelling

Cloisonné enamelling gets its name from the French word *cloison*, compartment. This technique involves attaching silver wire to metal with silver solder to form compartments. These compartments are then filled with enamel and fired in a kiln.

The simplest method is to counter-enamel the blank back. When cool, clean the side that has not been enamelled, to remove fire scale and restore it to a clean, bright finish. Apply a coat of enamel to the face. Draw out the wire and form into the shapes desired. Paint water onto the enamelled face and place the wire shapes on it. The water will keep the wire in place.

Place piece in kiln, and fire. Be sure that the wires stay flat on the blank. Tap them into the molten enamel, if necessary. Remove from kiln and allow to cool. Brush off any scaling, in preparation for adding the enamels. Both opaque and transparent enamels can be used.

Prepare the enamel by mixing it with water. The water will be cloudy. Pour it off and keep adding more until it runs clear. (This will prevent minute particles of enamel from rising to the surface after they are positioned in the compartments.) Pour off most of the water.

Use a small spatula and fill in each compartment carefully, pushing the enamel into all corners to expel air. Level the enamel with the top of the wire. Dry in front of the kiln to remove moisture. Finally, dry out on top of the kiln. Place inside the kiln when ready to fire.

In perfect work, enamel and wire are level. If necessary, add another layer of enamel and fire again. Alternatively, rub down the wire with a water of Ayr stone. Should it scar the enamel, fire very briefly to restore glaze. Clean piece with a cleaner or mild acid.

Champlevé

Champlevé involves etching a blank to create recesses into which wet enamel is placed. Etching is often done with acid, but soft metals need only scraping. A coating of flux is not necessary. After firing, enamel sometimes sits too high on a piece. If so, rub down on a stone when cool and return to the kiln for a short re-glaze.

Plique à Jour

This method is quite different from cloisonné and champlevé, and much more complicated. The basic idea is to fill holes and slots in a blank with enamel, rather like stained glass. The size of the holes and slots must not be too big, and metal should be of at least 18-gauge thickness.

Cut, clean, and thoroughly anneal a blank. Rest a sheet of mica on a thin plate of fireclay brick that is on a firing stand. Lay the clean blank on the mica. Prepare enamel as for cloisonné, but use only transparent enamels. Fill each hole or slot so full that it is domed. Shrinkage will bring the level down so that it is uniform with the metal. Do not place any enamel on the metal.

Dry *very* slowly. Take care not to overfire, but bring enamel to a good gloss. Let cool. If necessary, add more enamel, and refire. Overheating may cause enamel to flow over to the underside of the metal. When the piece has cooled, remove mica by breaking it off. Pickle the work in a weak solution of sulphuric acid. When cleaning, be careful not to bend the metal or the enamel may split.

Transfers

Enamel transfers are designs that have been printed onto a paper backing. A transfer is floated on water to remove the backing, then carefully lifted onto a fully enamelled blank. White or light tints make the best background for this work. Check that the transfer is color-side-up. Use blotting paper or tissue to press it firmly into the surface of the enamel. If possible, place in a cold kiln, and heat. If not, place in a 650° C kiln until glossy. Do not overheat, or the design may float into the base enamel.

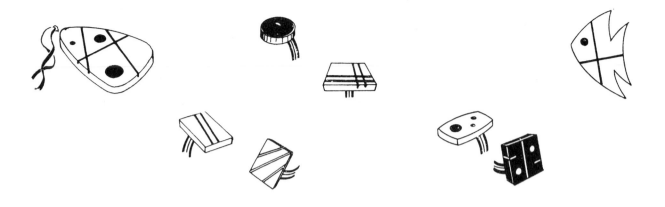

Illus. 243. Some silver jewelry designs.

APPENDIX B

SILVER JEWELRY

Silver is one of the most attractive metals, but in its pure form it is very soft and wears easily. In its most common use today, silver is sterling, or standard, which is 925 parts silver and 75 parts copper. The copper hardens the silver and improves its toughness. Where considerable manipulation of silver is necessary, as in bending, pure silver must be used.

Silver is available in a wide variety of forms, to satisfy most jewelers' needs. Casting silver is the most important. Sheet silver and silver wire are used widely in jewelrymaking. Sheets vary in thickness from .30 mm to 3.20 mm. Wires range from 0.51 mm to 19.00 mm. Useful, particularly in cloisonné enamelling, is round section tube.

Silver can be joined with silver solder. Five grades are available: extra soft, soft, medium, hard, and enamelling solder. Whenever a number of soldering stages occur in one job, always begin with the hardest solder.

Enamelling solder is probably the most difficult to use. It is confined to work that will be enamelled. Speak to a jeweler to find out which of the commercial brands of flux is the best to use with this type of solder. Hard solder is ideal for close joint work, due to its deep penetration qualities. Borax is a suitable flux to use with hard solder. Medium solder, just a grade above easy, is useful when a number of joints have already been made. Soft solder is used when a number of other solder joints have been made and it is important to keep the heat down to avoid disturbing the work.

Cuttlebone Casting

The cuttlefish has a hard, protective shell that can be used to cast silver. The bone is oval-shaped, and can be 250 mm in length, or longer. Cuttlebones can be picked up on the seashore, or purchased in pet shops or from jewelry suppliers or enamellists. The bone is easily carved, and has a texture that enhances the designs of castings.

Place the prepared design on paper ready for transfer to the bone. Carefully cut the bone in half, and sand the flat face, to produce a perfectly smooth, flat surface. Take a charcoal block of similar size, and rub bone and block together to mate the surfaces perfectly. Using the paper transfer as a guide, cut out the design with a knife. Cut a sprue in the end of the bone and broaden it to serve as a pouring gate. Cut a similar sprue and gate in the charcoal block. Wire both blocks together. Heat the metal and carefully but quickly pour it into the bone. When cool, remove from the mould, saw off the sprue, and file the edges carefully. Polish if necessary.

Brown and Sharpe Wire Gauge
(*Shown Actual Thickness*)

B & S Gauge	Metal Thickness	Sheet & Wire (diameter)	
12	0.0808 inches	12	
14	0.0641 ''	14	
16	0.0508 ''	16	
18	0.0403 ''	18	
20	0.0320 ''	20	
22	0.0253 ''	22	
24	0.0201 ''	24	
26	0.0159 ''	26	

Table 1.

Illus. 244. Box in European boxwood.

APPENDIX C

WOOD

Wood, the most important material for the items in this book, and one of our most precious resources, is often misused, wasted, and ignored. Many colorful, decorative woods are small in size. They are not commercially viable, and are rarely seen. So that everyone may enjoy this beauty, search out woods and experiment with them. When I take a small bush or shrub from the garden and there is only a lump of root or a stump, I dry it and carve or turn it. Roots produce interesting grain and often some exciting colors.

Many books have been written about wood and wood technology. I do not intend to add to the facts and figures, but I would like to offer my experience with various woods, and give some personal details that may be of interest.

BOXWOOD. One of the most beautiful woods to turn is box (*buxus sempervirens*). By means of sharp tools, superb, almost endless, shavings spiral off in a golden rain, leaving a perfectly smooth and shiny surface. On the bench, however, it can be nearly impossible to get a perfect finish.

Boxwood grows small, its grain interlocks, and the little knots give trouble. One of the best and easiest substitutes is Pau Marfin. It has very few knots, is a beautiful butter-yellow color, and is used widely. Years ago, Marples, a well-known edge-tool manufacturer, would not use boxwood unless it was butter-yellow and perfectly free of knots.

Illus. 245. Jewelry box of zebra-wood with English holly lid.

HOLLY. Comparable to box in texture is holly. It produces the whitest wood in the United Kingdom. Welsh holly is whiter than English, which is understandable if you are a Welshman. It is a slow-growing tree, and never grows to any real size. It is often found in hedgerows, and too often applauded for its festive, decorative qualities and ignored for everything else.

Holly is truly a beautiful wood under an edge tool. I use it a great deal for small work and inlaying. If I cut down a holly, I would saw it up and then naturally season it very slowly. I would also leave the bark on, paint the ends and branch ends, and not have the stickers too thick. I recently received a piece of Florida holly. It is rather different from English holly, being a dull pink.

ROSEWOOD. This is a wood that everyone seeks and many consider the ultimate in beauty. It is great for inlaying in lighter woods, but is expensive. Rio is far more beautiful than Indian, having more deep red and black. It is grand to work, but it has an oily secretion that often gums up tools, particularly boring tools. You can polish it well with your fingers, but I do not suggest you do this with the lathe on, or you will have burning, not turning.

Illus. 246. Box in ash with rose-wood lid. Holly insert in lid.

EBONY. I was in Canada a few years ago, and on my return home my hand luggage consisted of one briefcase and a chunk of ebony. This was given to me by a gentleman in the West. The check-in clerk was somewhat doubtful about the carry-on, but in no way was I going to be separated from this priceless piece. I admired it for a long time, and was almost afraid to cut it. I am mean with it, like some of my ancestors in West Wales. It is a delight to use, if somewhat brittle at times. I have used it in small inlay work and for tiny additions to my woodturning.

BOG OAK. Ebony brings to mind bog oak. This wood only appears in England, so I guess we don't have bogs in Wales (not that sort, anyway). This wood often comes up in the fields in the low-lying area around the Wash in East Anglia. It also comes out of the sea bed in the Grimsby area of Lincolnshire. These are buried tree trunks that have been preserved for hundreds of years.

Bog oak has all the features of oak, but it is black or dark grey, having been dyed in the soil. It cuts and turns like box, only better, leaving a beautiful surface enhanced by silver medullary flashes. It is rarely seen, and greatly prized. I lock mine in the safe and put the money in the garage. (Needless to say, I don't have much of the latter.)

BUBINGA. When I visited the United States, I had the great pleasure of being invited to look around one of the early cutlery manufacturers in New England. It was most revealing. The handles of the cutlery were bubinga, maple, and several other woods. I had used bubinga on handles many years before—had admired its color and the beauty of its grain.

Bubinga is a huge tree. The trunk can be up to 3 feet (.9144 m) across and upwards of 20 to 30 feet (6 m to 9 m) long. Years ago, in the factory I visited, they sawed the wood into shorter lengths and exploded them, instead of sawing them. I wonder what the OSHA people would think of that. Many of these trees grow in the most inaccessible places and never become veneer or lumber. A carving tool manufacturer in England has recently substituted bubinga for rosewood, due to the difficulty of obtaining rosewood in the United Kingdom.

COCOBOLO. Many years ago, in the heart of Sheffield, I was intrigued to hear the buzz of a circular saw. Filled with curiosity, I followed the sound and discovered a man standing on a mound of beautifully colored sawdust, sawing small pieces of wood in a tiny workshop thick with sawdust. I later discovered that these were the handles for the knives that Sheffield manufacturers so proudly made in those days.

Have you ever tried to signal a man hellbent on sawing wood, or grown hoarse with shouting, or prayed that break-time would come, or that the bell would sound the completion of a day? Well, I have. Eventually, when I felt that the only way this fellow would stop working was if he were to fall off his sawdust or suffocate in it, he looked up and saw me. "What, here?" he said in surprise. I was relieved, since I had begun to think that he was just a scruffy robot.

He turned out to be a wonderful source of knowledge about wood. In his time, he cut many exotic woods, and enjoyed most of them. He handled his saw better than he did his wife, I bet, and, unlike many wood sawyers, he had all his fingers. He was converting cocobolo, a wood I rarely see, and gave me a bag of offcuts. They were small, but grand for small stuff.

While travelling a few years back, I received a small plank of cocobolo from my good friend Dr. Donald Gallup of Sherwood Park, Alberta. I had it wrapped in the House of Tools, Calgary, and carried it home in triumph, without the permission of Air Canada. It is the most beautiful wood to work, hard under the cutting edge, but with an unbelievably good finish. I am looking for a guy with a tree.

WALNUT. People talk of walnut almost in hushed whispers, especially English walnut, since there is so little of it. In the United States there is that most beautiful American black walnut. The first of this I ever used came from the case of an American organ, which a friend of mine had sworn to burn (since he could not sell it) if I didn't take it away. I have since cultivated other friendships with people in the United States who are equally kind, if somewhat misguided in having me among their friends.

The most beautiful walnut I have used is Circassian walnut. It grows in Circassia, in the Caucasus. It has been said that this was the first of the walnuts to appear commercially. It is light brown, particularly in the sapwood, and has large areas of black, and black streaks. Circassian walnut machines beautifully, and cuts and turns like a dream. I acquired some slabs from a veneer manufacturer. Although they were short, they were fairly wide. It really was a wood to be enjoyed.

LABURNUM. I am an awful fellow. I talk too much; I admire things that I cannot afford; I lust after exotic woods in the same way that my wife lusts after perfume. I have been known to suggest to folks that particular trees spoil their gardens and should be cut down, really in the hope of having the trees given to me for wood. These terrible crimes I commit in the cause of woodcraft will, I hope, be forgiven by the Master Craftsman.

Illus. 247. Box in English walnut inlaid with white and dyed sycamore.

So many trees are grown in the garden and hedgerow. In spite of having such grand timber, they are ignored. In my garden grows a laburnum. It is called the golden chain tree, since it has a chain-like loop of yellow flowers. I calculate that if I live to be about one hundred, it will give me some beautiful wood. The heartwood is golden brown. The sapwood, which is very thin, is yellow. Upon exposure to light and air, the sapwood stays yellow, but the heartwood deepens to a superb deep rich brown. It doesn't grow to any size, but it certainly is worth looking at. It is the tree of the hedgerow in West Wales. Scottish laburnum is greenish brown and has a thicker bark. It's colder up there!

Illus. 248. Box in laburnum with sycamore lid with inlaid cabochon.

APPLE. Fruit trees yield excellent wood, particularly for turning. Apple is probably the best. It is much prized for the rich color of its heartwood and the superb finish it gives with edge tools. Before the Second World War, Henry Disston, that most outstanding saw-making company, made all their best handles of apple.

CHERRY. Cherry has probably given me the greatest pleasure among the fruit trees. In the 1950's I acquired a whole wild cherry (*Gean*). It was fairly large, though nothing like the size some of them grow to in the United States. It is very similar to black cherry (*Prunus serotina*), which grows in the Eastern United States. It is tough to cut, but produces a lovely surface and a color that does not fade.

PEAR. Don't ignore the damson, the plum, the peach, the almond, or the pear. They are all very good to work, and all have flashes of beautiful color. Pear wood was used at one time to manufacture drawing instruments. Its pale pink color and long, close grain made it ideal for set squares and tri-squares.

OAK. What can I say about oak? It carried nations to war, cradled the newly born, and housed the elderly in their final resting places. Oak has everything, no matter which one it is, the milder Japanese, the tougher American red, the unusual American white, or the toughest of all, the European.

I used to live near a pub some years ago that was rebuilt. The architect

Illus. 249. Ring box in brown oak with sycamore lid. Box and lid both have inlays.

in charge of the work bought an entire brown oak tree. The bar, all the doors, and the pub chairs and tables were made from it.

It is said that the oak likes two hundred years to grow, two hundred years to stand and be admired, and two hundred years to die. Once cut up, it will last forever. Stand at the foot of a mature oak, and wonder at the tales it might tell of the times it has stood through.

One of the very toughest oaks I have ever worked with is the holm oak. This is the only evergreen oak to grow in the United Kingdom. Apparently introduced here from the Mediterranean in the sixteenth century, it is a lovely tree and generally used only ornamentally. The wood is really tough, and has very short medullary rays, not unlike the Australian silky oak, sometimes referred to as lacewood. The latter, incidentally, turns beautifully.

PLANE. Talking of lacewood reminds me of the London plane. It was planted in London and other large cities because of its willingness to grow in the grimy and sooty atmosphere created in the old wood- and coal-fire days. It produces a much-despised wood, rarely seen commercially and never in furniture. Its color is not of great interest, but when the tree is quarter sawn, it shows the most beautiful lace form in the medullary, pale pink on a light background. I remember as a youngster travelling occasionally by the Great Western Railway in South Wales. At that time, the carriages were lined with veneered plywoods. Lacewood was one of them.

Veneers remind me of my misspent youth, but also of one better-spent day when I saw the *Queen Mary* in her maiden year. This fantastic piece of British skill used vast quantities of fine wood in her fittings and thousands of square feet of exotic veneers. To recognize them all, one would really need to be an expert. The tour was a great experience for this alone. I saw the ship again, just before she was sold. In spite of having been used as a troop carrier, as well as having carried thousands of passengers the woods were all as good-looking as ever.

YEW. Although classified botanically as a softwood, the yew itself is quite hard. It can be very cross-grained, and can have numerous cracks and splits. It grows often to a greater age than the oak. The yew is the tree of the ornamental garden, and can be clipped and shaped. It is

Illus. 250 (top). Box in Osage orange with English yew lid.

Illus. 251 (bottom). Small box in English yew with inlaid panel of wild flowers.

also the tree of the churchyard. Tale has it that it was planted in churchyards to prevent animals from being poisoned by the seeds of the fruit.

In West Wales there is a churchyard at Nevern that has a tale to tell. Inside the gate, there is an avenue of yew trees probably six to seven hundred years old. Rich, red blood flows from the trunk of the third yew on the right. Actually, it's sap. History says that several centuries ago, a priest was accused of a terrible crime. He protested his innocence right up to the time of his execution. Finally he proclaimed that the yews in the churchyard would bleed for the rest of time as a lasting reminder of his innocence. One of them still does.

Irish yew, in particular, because it is cultivated and grows long and straight, was used for bows. It is difficult to season, but even the small branches can be used for inlays and small work. Younger trees are used for veneers. Some very expensive furniture is veneered in yew.

SERVICE. Another tree frequently planted in private parks in the United Kingdom but never used for furniture is the service tree. I once had a piece and inquired its origin of a parson friend. (Even the clergy would speak to me at one time.) He referred me to the sawmills at Burghley House, Stamford, the home of the Marquis of Exeter.

Not knowing my place, but actively pursuing my need for wood knowledge, I ingratiated myself with the Estate Manager, and finally had the great pleasure of meeting the Marquis, the grandfather of the present Earl. He was a lovely man and showed me round those beautiful gardens laid out by Capability Brown. His knowledge of the trees was extraordinary. The Estate records revealed the planting date, origin, and species of every mature tree on the estate.

He pointed out the tree I was looking for, the *Pyrus sorbus domestica*. Its flowers have a very strong smell, and its wood is reddish brown. It cuts well and looks almost tropical in form. The wild service tree growing in Wales is said to have provided a cure for the colic, an illness now blessedly of the past. (You can believe that if you want, but it was my old granny who told me.)

LINDEN. Incidentally, to visit Burghley is to step back in time to Elizabeth I. For the wood craftsman, that is a special treat. Here are some of the most beautiful of carvings, many from the school of Grinling Gibbons. Most of the carvings are in English lime, the linden tree of that famous street, the *Unter den Linden* in East Berlin. The wood is superb for carving. Its grain is not strongly featured; it grows to a good length; it is even textured and largely without knots. It cuts easily and cleanly with sharp tools, leaving a fine finish. It was the favorite wood for making hat blocks in the old days, and was reputedly the best for piano keys. North American basswood has similar qualities.

IMBUIA. A wood that appeared in England just after the war is imbuia, better known as Brazilian walnut. It is not a walnut at all. It appears in large sizes, and is an interesting and exciting wood, because of its color variations. It ranges from yellow to deep chocolate brown. A most interesting feature is the presence of black streaks that appear almost like stains across the wood. Carefully season Brazilian walnut, and wear a mask if the wood is turned or sanded, since the dust can be irritating to the nose.

During a lecture-demonstration, I once bored a piece on the lathe. The waste piled up in the throat of the machine tool cutter and there was a fire on the lathe. The smoke gave off a most spicy scent, but my audience had to be recalled from a distance down the road to see the completed demonstration. It is the only time I have ever had a fire on the lathe, though it could happen anytime, since the shavings stick together and block the boring tool.

HORNBEAM. One of the most beautiful woods for finishes is hornbeam. This tree grows to a good size in Europe and North America, particularly Canada. Some years ago, a friend of mine called to say that he was bringing me a trunk of walnut. This arrived in my absence and was taken to Walt, the chief sawyer who usually sorted my wood. Some days later Walt called my office and said, "That walnut tree of yours, I have sawn it into five fine planks of hornbeam."

I have made some beautiful handles of hornbeam. It is a hard, creamy-white wood. When turned, it gives a perfectly polished surface. Many old craftsmen turned their tool handles from it. Hornbeam was also used to make screws for old-type wooden vises. Even now, German plane manufacturers add a hornbeam sole to their beech plane bodies.

TABEBUIA. Ken Keusch, a doctor friend of mine (it's a good idea to have one around), sent me some twenty different woods from his home in Florida. (He wasn't showing off; he's just a really nice guy.) Among the woods was one I had used many years before. I knew it as *Pau d'arco*, but he called it *Tabebuia*. It is a dark golden brown, with a greenish tinge. The pieces were greatly figured, and there were many variations of broken grain. I used it on some small caskets that came out very beautifully, but I did have some trouble with the finishing.

PARTRIDGE. In the late 1940's, I took my wife and children to Wells-Next-the-Sea, in Norfolk, for an annual holiday. When the children weren't burying daddy in the sand (my wife often wished they would—completely), I wandered around, discovering the place. As usual, I was attracted to a machine noise, sorted out the place of origin, and found a man with a lathe. All around him were stacks of sawn wood about 1¾-inch (4.44-cm) square and 2 feet (.6-m) long, that were going to be turned into South African police truncheons. The wood was partridge, and was a beautiful, deep chocolate-brown. It was long-grained, very hard, and *very* heavy. I came away with some reject pieces, and turning them was a complete delight. I have never bettered the polish turning them gave.

LIGNUM VITAE. I was always intrigued when I read books or articles on *treen*, particularly when reference was made to wassail bowls made of lignum vitae. It wasn't until I joined my last employer that I had the opportunity to use this wood. The name relates to a drug, and the wood has more uses than any other known wood. It has a resin-gum content that makes it self-lubricating. Its sapwood is yellow, and sometimes it is used as a substitute for box. Its color is greenish black at the heart, and it darkens on exposure to light and air.

Turning and machining lignum vitae is a delight. Its close grain, together with its gum, makes it easy to obtain a superb finish. Unfortunately, it is difficult to get large pieces, and I have never had the opportunity to make anything of any real size.

TULIP. Recently, I was asked to turn some lace bobbins in tulipwood. The color is most unusual—yellow with varying shades of orange, red, and purple stripes. The wood was a little brittle, but turning it was a dream, and the machine finish was excellent.

AILANTHUS. Yes, I am one of the most fortunate men, inasmuch as friendly people give me wood, knowing my love of it. Occasionally, I am given a "pup," as it were. A friend gave me a sackful of *Ailanthus altissima*. This wood closely resembles ash, but its grain is straight. Its straightness is probably the attraction for the woodworker. I have found when working this wood, that interior splits only revealed in cutting suddenly appear. You cannot see them from end splits, so beware. It is really quite a useless wood.

ELM. A wonderful Scot who works for the Earl of Linlithgow on his estate in South Queensferry is one of the most knowledgable men I know when it comes to wood. Recently, a huge elm had to be felled on the estate, and a burl 3 feet (.91 m) across and some 14 inches (35.5 cm) deep was cut from the trunk. A 2-inch (5.08-cm) piece was saved for me.

Thus began for me a new dimension in carving. Nature's carvings are far better than mine. The exterior reveals beautiful and intriguing shapes that would make even Gibbons envious. The wood inside is also an adventure into the unknown. In spite of non-directional grain, grit, and dirt, the finish obtained with a plane and other edge tools is high-quality. The burl turns equally well. The block stays together, and the final finish is superb, in spite of the holes and cracks common to burls.

CHESTNUT. The trees at Linlithgow must be seen to be believed. I saw a Spanish chestnut twenty feet (6 m) long and seven feet (2 m) in diameter on the ground waiting for an intrepid lumberman to move it to a mill. A standing Spanish chestnut has a trunk carved by nature second to none. I often wonder how many beautiful trees there are on private estates, rarely seeing the sight of man or giving him pleasure.

Illus. 252. Jewelry box in elm burl with turned lid.

APPENDIX D

GLUES

Glues can be divided into three groups: those for general bonding of wood, those for bonding wood and other materials, and those for attaching laminated plastic sheet.

General Bonding

Animal glue is still popular, and is the best answer for some woodworking applications, such as veneering. Scotch glue, as it is generally known, is made of gelatin from the bones and hides of animals. It is available in cake, powder, or pearl form, and is mixed with water and heated in the top of a double boiler. It must never be boiled, and should flow continuously and easily from the brush.

Fish glue is a more refined product. It is generally sold in small tubes. It can be used for most woodworking jobs, but would be expensive to use in large quantities.

Casein glue is milk protein mixed with caustic soda and hydrated lime. It sells as a powder that is mixed with an equal quantity of water. Casein glue tends to leave a dark black stain on woods containing tannic acid.

Polyvinyl acetate glues are cold-setting glues. They are usually found in the form of a thick white emulsion. P.V.A. can be used for most woodworking jobs, but should not be used in damp environments.

Illus. 253. Gluing a bangle: Laminated block and glue chuck being spread with hot-melt glue.

Illus. 254. Block and chuck clamped in wood vise.

Bonding Wood and Other Materials

Epoxy-resin glue can be used to bond almost anything. It is a syrupy mixture of equal parts of adhesive and hardener. Individually, the parts have a long shelf life. Once mixed, the glue has a short setting period, which can be made even shorter with moderate heat.

Synthetic resin glues were largely developed in the period immediately prior to World War II. Bonding plywood and other wood forms, in the production of planes like the Mosquito, demanded a strong, moisture-proof glue. Aero research in England developed a glue using a urea formaldehyde formula. A large number of variations of this basic glue are now available for bonding most materials. Generally these glues require hardeners. The chemical reaction of the hardener and the resin produces the bond. This glue can also be used as a gap filler.

Bonding Laminated Plastic Sheets to Wood

To attach plastic laminates to wood requires an entirely different type of glue. These are rubber-based glues and must be applied to both sides. Bonding is immediate, so the component parts must be attached very accurately at the outset.

APPENDIX E

EQUIPMENT TO MAKE

Abrasive Tools

Sandpaper (glass paper) is extremely useful for finishing on the bench and in the lathe. Sanding at the bench can be made easier by wrapping ¼-inch (6.35-mm) sheets of sandpaper (glass paper) around cork blocks. Improve blocks by gluing sandpaper (glass paper) to pieces of wood with different cross-sections, and cutting them approximately 9-inches (225-mm) long. The blocks can be used as files or rasps, depending on the abrasiveness of the paper (Illus. 255).

Illus. 255a. Woodblock to use for an abrasive stick.

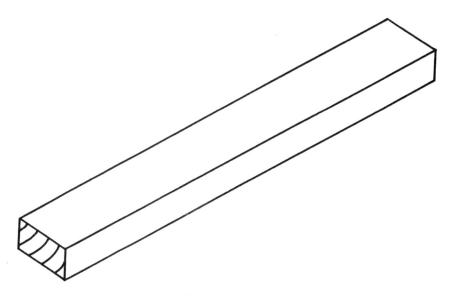

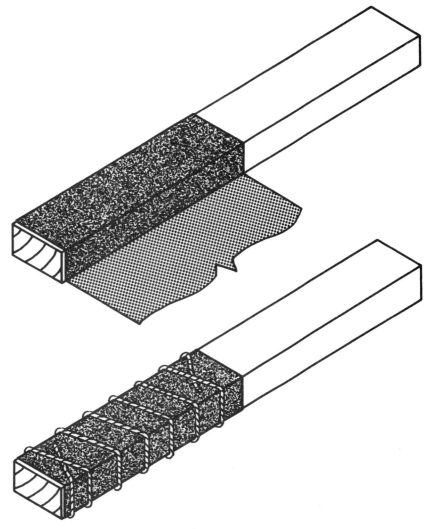

Illus. 255b. Wrapping sand-paper (glass paper) around the block.

Illus. 255c. Holding the sand-paper (glass paper) with string until the glue dries.

Use an abrasive board when it is necessary to keep sanded surfaces completely flat. Glue whole sheets of sandpaper (glass paper) onto pieces of plywood or hardboard. Make several boards at a time, using different grades of paper (Illus. 256a–256c).

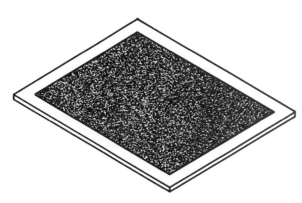

Illus. 256a. Simple abrasive board.

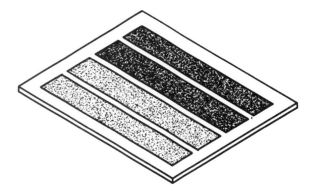

Illus. 256b. Abrasive board with strips of varying grades of sandpaper (glass paper).

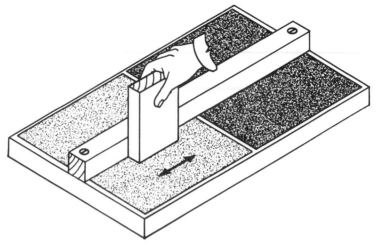

Illus. 256c. Abrasive board with center upstand.

Make abrasive spindles and use them on the lathe or in the drill. They are helpful for sculptural work and jobs that are held underneath the spindle. Suit the shape of the spindle to the job it will serve.

Lathe-mounted spindles are made of pieces of dowel or wood shaped on the lathe and covered with sandpaper (glass paper). They make excellent sculpting and finishing tools (Illus. 257–259).

Illus. 257. Abrasive spindle mounted on the lathe.

Illus. 258. Abrasive spindle in use shaping a piece of costume jewelry.

Illus. 259. Abrasive spindles for use between centers on the lathe.

Abrasive drums can be drill-mounted and used with the drill hand-held or mounted on the bench (Illus. 260–261).

Illus. 260. Tapered abrasive spindle for use in the electric drill.

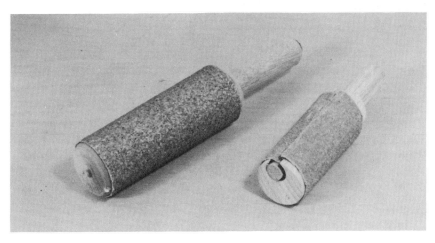

Illus. 261. Abrasive spindles for use in the electric drill.

Bench Tools

A lipped work board is particularly useful for holding thin material for planing, or for working with other tools. The job can be held with folding wedges against the shallow lip. Low-relief panels can be held firmly this way (Illus. 262–263).

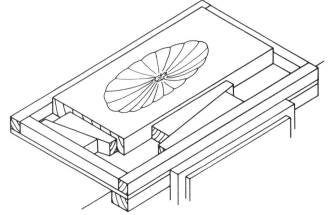

Illus. 262. Lipped work board with wedges.

Illus. 263. Abrasive board with upstand all around can be used as a lipped work board.

A manufactured bench hook may well be inadequate for sawing, particularly for an inexperienced user. Make an improved version, fitting it with an upstand that extends the full width of the hook and gives adequate support to both ends of the wood being sawn. The board has greater stability because of its greater width (Illus. 264).

Make a small wood vise, using the folding-wedge principle. It can be used on the bench top and is particularly helpful with planing, sawing, and carving (Illus. 265).

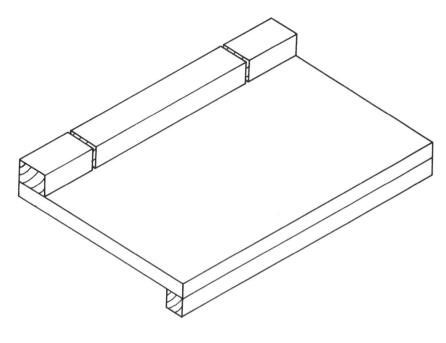

Illus. 264. Improved bench hook.

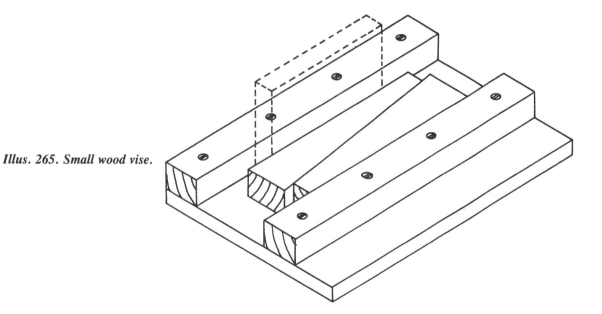

Illus. 265. Small wood vise.

Hold dowels for sawing in a bench hook equipped with a pair of folding wedges or a round rod held in a v-grip. Use a renewable insert, to give the jig a longer life (Illus. 266).

For a planing cradle for dowels, use the same principle as for the sawing jig, but fit a stop. Flats can be planed on the dowel rod with this device (Illus. 267).

For accurate planing, particularly of end grain, it is a good idea to make a small shooting board. Beechwood is a good choice, because it wears evenly and can be used with accuracy.

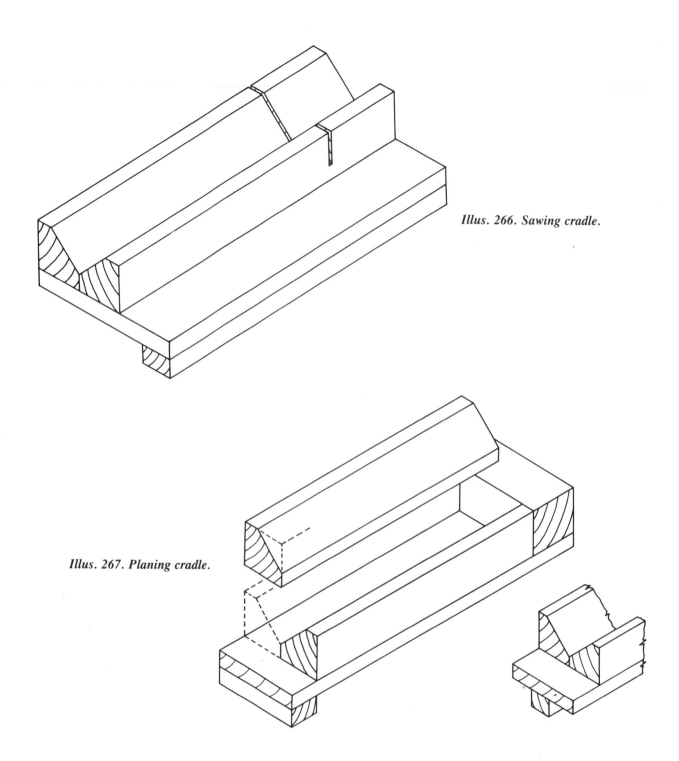

Illus. 266. Sawing cradle.

Illus. 267. Planing cradle.

All these aids can be fitted with a block on the underside and held securely in the vise (Illus. 268). Alternatively, they can be fitted with two ½-inch (12.7-mm) dowels set on 7-inch (175-mm) centers, 2 inches (50 mm) in from the front edge. Bore two ½-inch (12.7-mm) holes in the middle of the top of the bench. Each device can be located instantly and held securely in this way.

Illus. 268. Folding wedge bench vise with full-length upstand and hardwood insert to save wear.

Illus. 269. Record 414 vise with rear jaw removed and wooden jaw substituted.

Boring Aids

Wood bored by hand or with an electric drill must be held in a vise. Wherever possible, particularly if accuracy is of prime importance, mount the electric drill on a bench stand. Many types are available. The prime requirements are rigidity and height and depth adjustability (to deal with woods of varying thicknesses and hole depths).

For boring holes, a machine vise is necessary. I have an inexpensive, strong vise, fitted with a non-lifting swivel jaw capable of holding awkwardly shaped work. Both fixed and moving jaws have vertical and horizontal faces. Vises should fit standard power-tool tables or bases. For woodworking, fit the jaws with wooden plates to protect the work. To hold more, remove the moving jaw and substitute a hardwood one (Illus. 269).

Holding small pieces of wood for boring can be a problem, especially if the pieces are round or irregularly shaped. The danger to hands and fingers when holding wood close to moving tools cannot be over-emphasized. A safe way to hold tiny pieces is to attach them to small scraps of wood, using the electric-glue gun. The glue holds firmly, but removes easily after boring.

Alternatively, it is easy to make a small hand vise, with v-cuts for holding curved and awkwardly shaped pieces. A single wedge or folding wedges will hold the work securely (Illus. 270).

A variation on the hand vise is one that can be gripped in the machine vise and eliminates any possibility of the boring tool being damaged by striking the metal jaws of the vise (Illus. 271).

Illus. 270. Wood hand vise with folding wedges to hold plug when boring.

Illus. 271. Wood vise with folding wedges holding block for boring.

APPENDIX F

HEAT TREATMENT OF WOODWORKING TOOLS

Recently, I had a woodcarving student from overseas who brought his own tools with him. It was evident almost immediately that a number of them were lacking the correct heat treatment and were failing to hold their edges. I had no means of testing or finding the Brinell hardness of his tools, but clearly they were not up to standard. I could, of course, have let him use my tools, and could have advised him to purchase a better set when he returned to his own country. However, I decided to add "Hardening and Tempering Tools" to the course content, and we both enjoyed this addition to our activities.

Heat-treating tools requires a good heat source that can be applied to the whole tool or a specific area of it. Heat can be applied with a blow torch, either the paraffin or cylinder type. Alternatively, a small steel cylinder heated over a gas ring can be used for small tools. Larger tools can rest on a sheet of steel placed over the burner of a large gas stove. Heat treating also requires oil or water contained in a small tin or drum, tongs for holding tools, and some fine emery cloth for brightening the metal. My torch is assembled to a cartridge holder with suitable controls. A small electric blower supplies the unit with air. The apparatus is reasonably priced and extremely efficient (Illus. 272–273).

When steel is heated, oxidation takes place and oxides appear on the surface of the metal. The oxides are of many hues, each depending on the temperature of the metal at that particular spot. These colors range

Illus. 272. Heat treatment bench: Flamefast torch, gas control, and small air blower. Note that the blade has been removed from the gouge handle.

Illus. 273. The torch is lit and the flame has been adjusted.

from very pale straw to brown, from purple to blue, and they move across the metal in fairly clearly defined bands. To see the colors clearly the metal should be bright, so this is a task best performed in broad daylight. Years ago, when tools were hardened and tempered individually, if a man had a badly tempered tool, it was often said that the weather must have been overcast on the day it was made.

Hardening and Tempering

All tools must first be hardened. With a pair of tongs, place tool in the torch flame. Apply heat about 3-inches (7.6-cm) from the cutting end

Illus. 274. Blade being heated to cherry red.

(Illus. 274). When the metal reaches cherry red, the temperature will be approximately 1700–1800 degrees F. (800–850 degrees C.). Quench in water or oil (Illus. 275). Hold the metal vertically in the liquid and cool rapidly. This will ensure hardness. A tool quenched in water will be much harder than one cooled in oil, since oil cooling tends to be slower. Old motor oil can be used in the oil bath. Use oil carefully. A small quantity can heat up rapidly and may well catch fire. Do not harden the entire tool, or the tang end will tend to be brittle. Be careful to avoid distorting the tool by unequal immersion.

Illus. 275. Cherry red blade being immersed in oil.

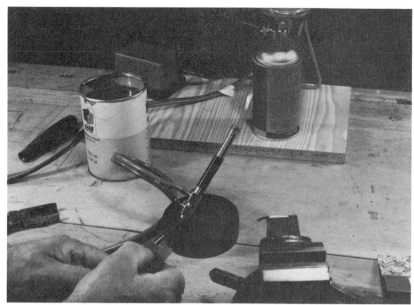

Illus. 276. The blade wiped dry and returned to its original brightness by being rubbed with an emery cloth.

When the tool is cool, wipe it dry and use the emery cloth to polish the first inch or so (Illus. 276). Next, carefully apply the blow-torch flame behind the polished area. After a very short time, a color band will appear and move along the tool away from the torch point, toward the cutting edge (Illus. 277). When a golden brown color appears at the edge, very quickly quench the tool. This halts the heat and will give the correct degree of hardness to the cutting edge. Clean tool with the emery cloth. Prepare handle and assemble, to complete the tool.

The foregoing can be applied to any tool where the degree of hardness is in doubt. Should a tool have its temper drawn, it can be re-tempered in this way.

Illus. 277. Heat being applied and colors running along the blade.

TEMPERING CHART (Carbon steel only)

Color		Temperature	Tools
Yellow	pale	428 °F. (194 °C.)	
	straw	446 °F. (202 °C.)	Keen edges—surgery tools
	golden	470 °F. (213 °C.)	Knives
Brown	golden	490 °F. (222 °C.)	Chisels, scissors
	purple	510 °F. (231 °C.)	Plane irons, adzes
Purple		530 °F. (240 °C.)	All other woodworking tools
Blue	bright	550 °F. (250 °C.)	
	full	560 °F. (254 °C.)	Saws and auger bits
	dark	600 °F. (272 °C.)	
Red			Softer if allowed to air-cool

Table 2.

Alloyed steel must be carefully and correctly tempered, since incorrect heat treatment may ruin it. To identify a piece of steel, grind it on a dry wheel. Whitish yellow sparks indicate plain carbon steel. The sparks tend to be close together. Dull red sparks indicate high-speed steel. The sparks scatter in all directions.

To ascertain the hardness of steel without using a machine, put a drop of nitric acid on the steel. This will produce a black spot. The lighter the spot, the softer the steel. The steel is not affected by the acid, but it is a good idea to wash it off after the test, and also to wash your hands.

APPENDIX G

TOOLS AND EQUIPMENT

Boring Tools

Sawtooth machine bits are versatile boring tools for the lathe or drill press. They are capable of boring deep or shallow holes, overlapping holes, or holes off the edge (Illus. 278).

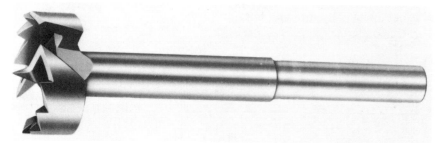

Illus. 278. Sawtooth machine bit.

Forstner machine bits are perfect for cutting accurate shallow holes in hard or soft wood. The holes can also be bored to overlap or run off the edge (Illus. 279).

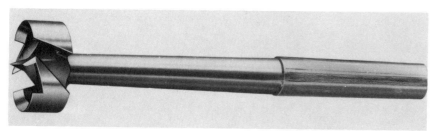

Illus. 279. Machine Forstner bit.

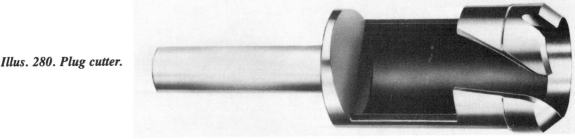

Illus. 280. Plug cutter.

Machine plug cutters must be used in the drill press (Illus. 280). This tool cuts polished plugs and ejects them from the side. An equally effective plug cutter, but without side ejection, is one manufactured by Fuller (Illus. 281).

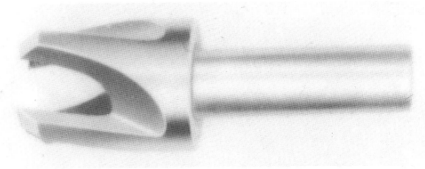

Illus. 281. Plug cutter.

A wood drill is similar to that used by the metalworker, except that it has a longer nose and an open flute to eject shavings easily (Illus. 282).

Illus. 282. Wood drill bit.

Illus. 283. Lip-and-spur drill bit.

Lip and spur drills, equipped with two spurs, cut perfect holes in both hard and soft woods (Illus. 283).

Lathe Equipment

The pin mandrel, one of the latest developments for the lathe, is an attachment that holds pre-bored wood. A small pin rests on a small flat on the mandrel and moves by centrifugal action to hold the work securely when the lathe is running (Illus. 284–285).

The collet chuck is designed on the same principle as the engineer's chuck, but with sprung jaws of different sizes to hold a variety of diameters (Illus. 286).

The expanding collet chuck holds large or small bowls, plates, platters, or boxes. The jaws expand as the ring is screwed down to fit tightly into a recess cut in the base of the work (Illus. 287). The expanding collet chuck can also be fitted with 1-inch (2.54-cm) jaws for smaller work (Illus. 288).

Illus. 284 (left). Pin mandrel or spigot chuck with knob blank assembled.

Illus. 285 (below). Pin mandrels in four sizes.

Illus. 286 (left). Collet chuck.

Illus. 287 (directly below). Expanding collet chuck.

Illus. 288 (bottom). Expanding collet chuck with smaller collet.

Illus. 289. Expanding collet six-in-one chuck.

A more versatile expanding collet chuck has nine different sizes of expanding collet. It has a split-ring facility and can also be used as a collar chuck. It can be converted to a screw chuck and the body also used as a faceplate. This is the world's most complete lathe-holding device (Illus. 289).

The screw chuck is ideal for holding small work for turning. The screw is replaceable and is adjustable for length. A larger chuck can be used as a faceplate, with holes pre-bored to receive screws (Illus. 290). The screw is an ordinary wood screw. A California manufacturer has a much improved screw that makes for accurate replacement of the work, should this be necessary. The holding and screwing qualities make it infinitely superior to any other currently available.

Illus. 290. Screw-nose chucks.

Cone drives can be screwed to the headstock of Coronet lathes or to a Morse tapered mandrel, to enable them to be used with any lathe. They can also be attached to some running centers, to provide running cones. These are great time savers, since they permit instant assembly of square or round stock to the lathe. They can also be used to turn quarters and halves (Illus. 291).

Screwed taper mandrels allow one manufacturer's lathes to be used with another's equipment (Illus. 292).

Illus. 291. Cone centers.

Illus. 292. Morse taper screw-nose adapters.

Illus. 293. Running centers with optional inserts.

This running center has a solid center that can be substituted for a cone center and an adaptor to facilitate cone assembly (Illus. 293).

The spigot chuck is among the latest in chucks (Illus. 294). The collet holds work by means of a small spigot cut on the end of the material. The spigot need not be over ¼ inch (6.35 mm). The spigot chuck can also be fitted with a pin mandrel and used to hold pre-bored material. The pin mandrel can also be used to keep the collet of the chuck in the rest position when not in use.

Illus. 294. Exploded spigot chuck, showing spanners and pin chuck.

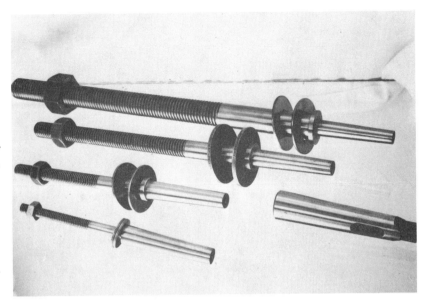

Illus. 295. Woodturning mandrels for wheels in various sizes.

Various size mandrels are available with a Morse taper for the headstock and countersunk at the right end to receive the running center of the tailstock. Sleeves can be fitted to convert number one Morse tapers to number two or number three. Ideal for wheels and other work with a center hole (Illus. 295).

Other Equipment

The woodworker's vise is a useful clip-on for smaller woodworking projects. It fits on a kitchen table or small shelf (Illus. 296).

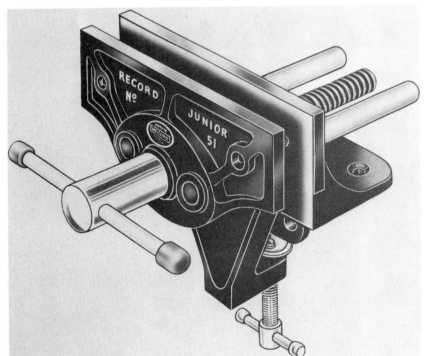

Illus. 296. Record clip-on vise that can be used anywhere.

Illus. 297. Zyliss Strongboy strapwrench, used to remove cones effortlessly.

The strap wrench can remove cones from the lathe. It can also be used to hold irregularly shaped pieces (Illus. 297).

The metalworking vise is a small clip-on. With replaceable jaws and a small anvil it is ideal for jewelry work and small metalwork projects. It can be fitted with specially made soft jaws when holding delicate work (Illus. 298).

Illus. 298. Record clip-on vise for jewelry and small metalwork.

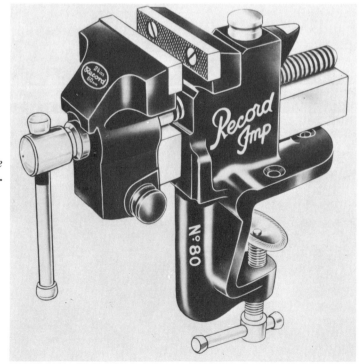

Enamelling Equipment

This enamelling kiln is gas fired (Illus. 299). It can be used with natural gas, or any of the bottled gases. It is fitted with piezo ignition and a temperature indication. It is one of the best in the area of small kilns, and is used with a variety of small tools (Illus. 300a–300d).

Illus. 300a.
Scrolling tool.

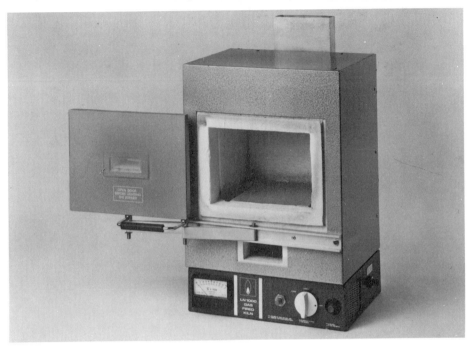

Illus. 299. Flamefast LN1000 Mk II gas-fired kiln.

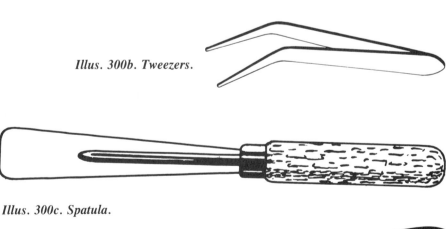

Illus. 300b. Tweezers.

Illus. 300c. Spatula.

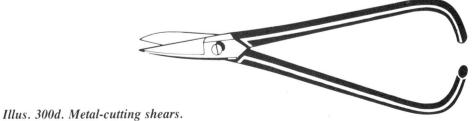

Illus. 300d. Metal-cutting shears.

A torch with an electric blower and disposable butane cartridges is superb for the small workshop or jeweler's bench. It can also be used for simple enamelling (Illus. 301–302).

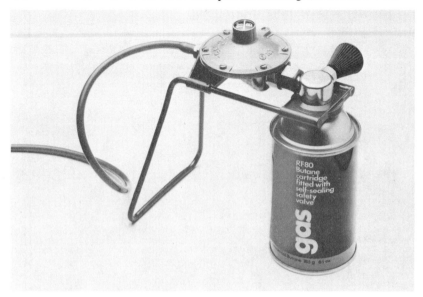

Illus. 301. Flamefast Porta-flame portable butane gas unit.

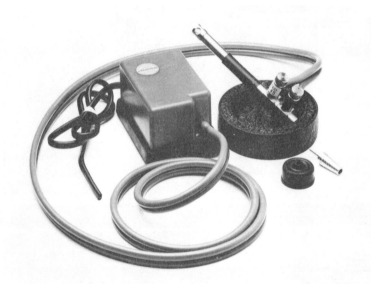

Illus. 302. Flamefast Needle-flame Torch Kit, with base, twined tubing, adapter, and air pump.

A GALLERY
OF
CONTEMPORARY WOODWORK

Illus. 303. Jewelry boxes by Ken Keusch in kokko (Albizzia lebbeck) with inlaid ceramic discs.

A GALLERY OF CONTEMPORARY WOODWORK

The following pages show the artwork of some contemporary craftsmen. All display a remarkable appreciation and use of material. I marvel at the mighty miniatures of Del Stubbs, that most painstaking and innovative California craftsman. The work of Dr. Owen D. Standen really must be seen to be appreciated. Standen, a former director of the Wellcome Research Institute, collected wood in journeys around the world. Upon retirement he took up woodcraft, and his inlaid turnings are truly astounding. Space does not permit a discussion here of each contributor's artistry, so the notes accompanying the photographs must suffice.

Illus. 304. Ring box in black walnut with cherry lid by Ken Keusch with enamel inlays by Thea Katzenstein.

Illus. 305.

Illus. 306 (right). Jewelry box by Ken Keusch in pink ivory with black ebony knob.

Illus. 307 (below). Jewelry chest by Ken Keusch cut with the bandsaw. Chest is black walnut, knob is black ebony. Enamelling by Audrey Komrad.

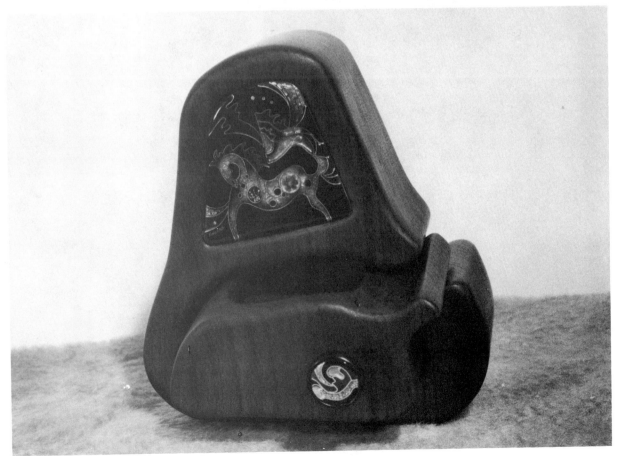

Illus. 308. Rosewood turning by Ken Keusch mounted on a blackwood base. Enamelling by Audrey Komrad.

Illus. 309. Jewelry box by Ken Keusch in kingwood with embossed top in African blackwood.

Illus. 310. Beautiful birds hand-carved by David Orchard using simple hand tools.

Illus. 311.

Illus. 312.

Illus. 313–314. Small box in rosewood by Ralph Stanford, a former pupil of John Sainsbury's, now in Tasmania. The location of the curve is unusual.

Illus. 313.

Illus. 314.

Illus. 315–316. Box in ash by Ralph Stanford.

Illus. 317–320. Miniature egg by Ralph Stanford in rosewood contained within another egg in ash.

Illus. 321–322. Chess set by William Beresford. The table is oak with mahogany squares.

Illus. 323. Natural topped African blackwood bowls by Ray Key.

Illus. 324. Natural topped burr elm bowls (left & right), and a soft knobbed thuja burr box (center) by Ray Key.

Illus. 325. Soft squat cocobolo box (left), soft, knobbed maisethorne box (center), and sun hat Brazilian tulipwood box (right) by Ray Key.

Illus. 326. Tall knobbed cocobolo box (left), Indian rosewood box (center), and voamboana box by Ray Key.

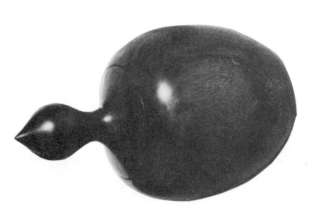

Illus. 327. Macassar ebony finial-knobbed box (left), paraking box (center), and Brazilian tulipwood box by Ray Key.

Illus. 328. Thimbles by Peter Stiles of Bristol. Woods from left to right are: oak, grand palisander, Brazilian tulipwood, and Indian ebony.

Illus. 329. Claro walnut container with yew inlay by Del Stubbs.

Illus. 330. Claro walnut container with spalted sycamore inlay by Del Stubbs.

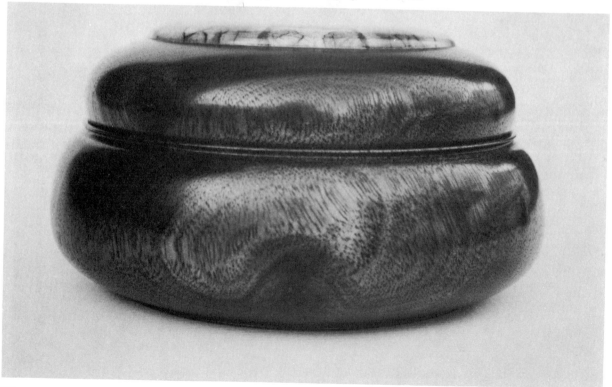

Illus. 331. Claro walnut container with myrtle inlay by Del Stubbs.

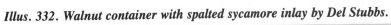

Illus. 332. Walnut container with spalted sycamore inlay by Del Stubbs.

Illus. 333. Bowl bottom. Bowl by Del Stubbs.

Illus. 334. Curly claro walnut bowl bottom. Bowl by Del Stubbs.

Illus. 335. Claro walnut bowl bottom. Bowl by Del Stubbs.

Illus. 336. Cocobolo rosewood container with lid by Del Stubbs.

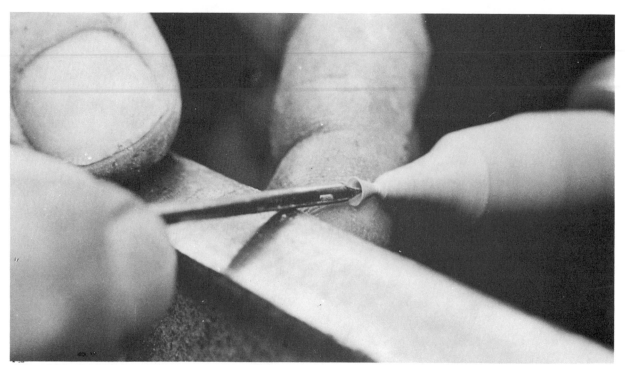

Illus. 337. Del Stubbs turning the top of a goblet in boxwood. Although greatly enlarged here, the top is ⁵/₃₂-inch (4-mm) tall. (Photo by Beth Erikson, Twin Butte, Alberta, Canada.)

Illus. 338. Del Stubbs sanding a yew vase carefully to maintain crisp lines and details. (Photo by Beth Erikson.)

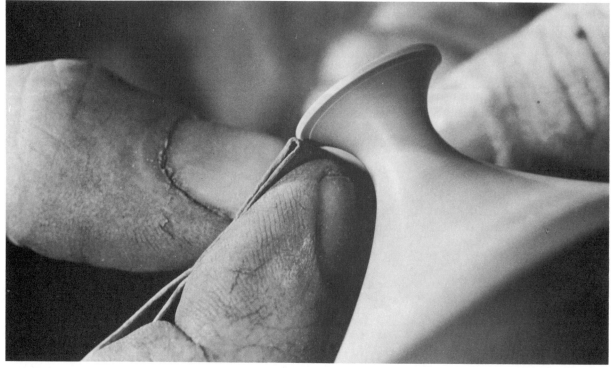

Illus. 339. English walnut vase by Del Stubbs.

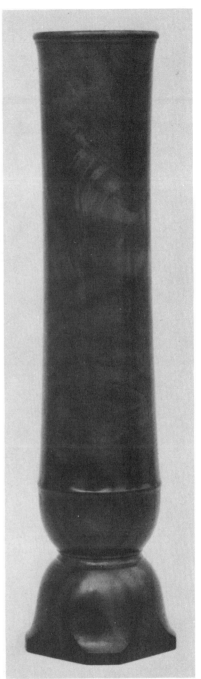

Illus. 340. Claro walnut vase by Del Stubbs.

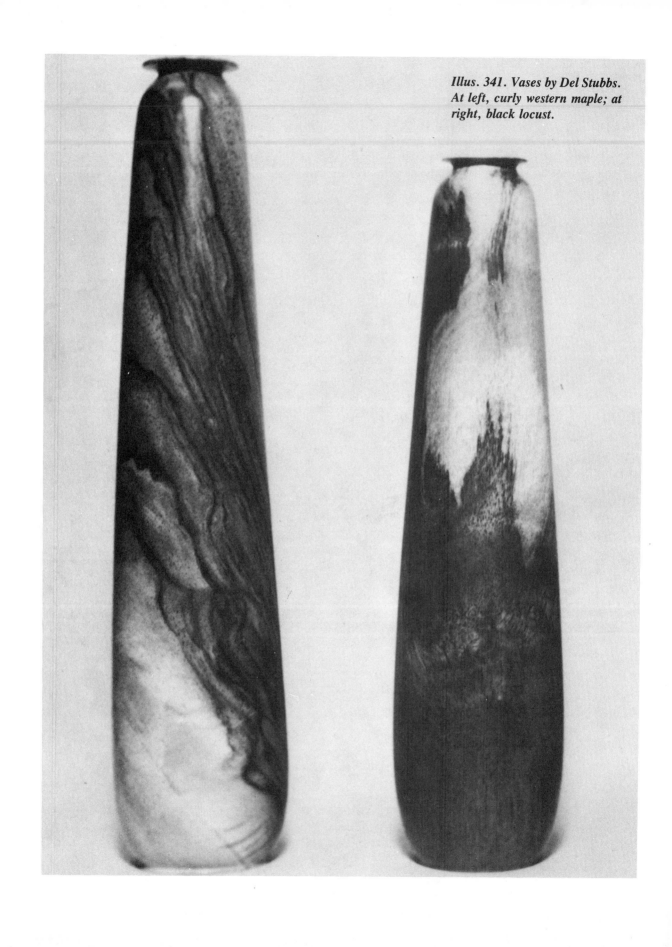

Illus. 342. Vases by Del Stubbs. At left, myrtle; at right, English walnut.

Illus. 343. Claro walnut container with spalted sycamore inlay by Del Stubbs.

Illus. 344. "Japanese landscape," a rosewood container with spalted sycamore inlay by Del Stubbs.

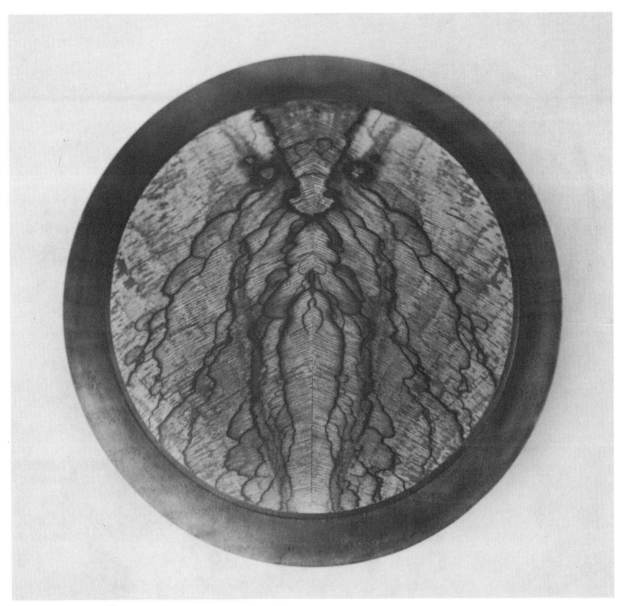

Illus. 345. "Old Merlin," a claro walnut container with spotted sycamore inlay by Del Stubbs.

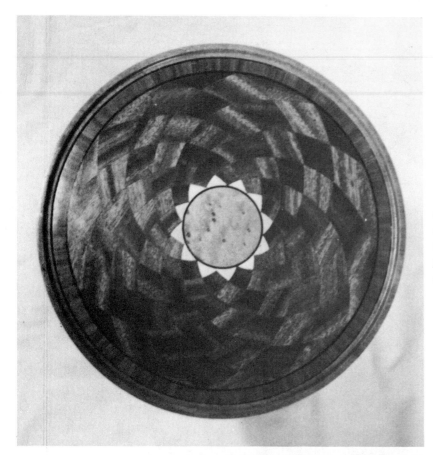

Illus. 346. Parquetry veneer tabletop by Tom Candler. The design is based on the marble floor pattern beneath the dome of Masta Church, Malta.

Illus. 347. Bowl turned and inlaid by Tom Candler.

Illus. 348. Inlaid plate by O. D. Standen.

Illus. 349. Inlaid plate by O. D. Standen.

Illus. 350. Inlaid box by O. D. Standen.

Illus. 351. Inlaid box by O. D. Standen.

Illus. 352. Inlaid box by O. D. Standen.

BIBLIOGRAPHY

Chinn, Garry, and Sainsbury, John. *The Garrett Wade Book of Wood-working Tools*. New York: Thomas Y. Crowell, Publishers, 1979.

Sainsbury, John. *The Complete Textbook of Woodturning*. New York: McGraw-Hill, Inc., 1979.

Sainsbury, John. *Sainsbury's Woodturning Projects for Dining*. New York: Sterling Publishing Co., Inc., 1981.

Illus. 353. Miniature digital clock in rosewood.

INDEX